C000259533

For Drena,

The author's dear friend.

Bri. Halliday
December 1995

Glenthorne

A MOST ROMANTIC PLACE

Glenthorne
A MOST ROMANTIC PLACE

U.J. HALLIDAY

EXMOOR BOOKS

First published in Great Britain in 1995 by Exmoor Books

Copyright © 1995 the estate of U.J. Halliday

All rights reserved. No part of this publication may be reproduced, stored in a retrieval system, or transmitted in any form or by any means electronic, mechanical, photocopying, recording or otherwise, without the prior permission of the copyright holder.

British Library Cataloguing-in-Publication Data
A CIP Catalogue Record for this book is available from the British Library

ISBN 0 86183 285 X

EXMOOR BOOKS
Dulverton, Somerset

Trade sales enquiries
Westcountry Books
Halsgrove House
Lower Moor Way
Tiverton, EX16 6SS

Telephone: 01884 243242
Facsimile: 01884 243325

Printed and bound in Great Britain by
Bookcraft Ltd., Midsomer Norton.

CONTENTS

FOREWORD

Ursula Halliday became the mistress of Glenthorne somewhat unexpectedly in 1968 but she had married into the family as early as 1950 and had already benefited from the confidences and reminiscences of the previous two generations. While she lived in the house, during the next sixteen years, she wondered, as many have done, who on earth could have decided to build a house there and why. What follows is the result of her researches into the family papers she discovered in attics and drawers. It may possibly prove useful to those who are interested in the recent history of the Exmoor area or in changing attitudes to landscape. Glenthorne House itself was sold in 1984 and the family moved to Ashton where the author built a library to preserve the books and papers. She died in 1992.

THE SETTING

I am at present sitting in a slightly crumbling monument to rural simplicity erected in the early nineteenth century when Romanticism was the only right thought and wild, unspoilt country the best stimulus for it. It is what might be described, in the language of the time at which it was built, as a commodious manor house – small as big houses go but huge, rambling and draughty as modern accommodation is understood.

It was started in the reign of King William IV and its style is extremely difficult to describe: 'transitional' and 'eclectic' are words that spring to mind. It is still classical Georgian in places and Gothic in others but it has a homeliness that is much more Tudoresque and foreshadows countless pleasant Victorian villas. It is a warm colour, built of pinkish local stone ornamented with Bath stone and roofed with Cornish slate, but it would be unremarkable, just another big house that had outlived its purpose, if it were not for its truly remarkable setting. Perched on a North Devon cliff on one of the few patches of flattish land there, it is surrounded by some of the grander scenery to be found in England – high hills seamed with combes and covered in thick woodland. It is difficult at first to see the track that winds down from the barren moorland above through nearly three miles of hairpin bends to the house lying in a sort of composed and cosy lunacy at the bottom.

One cannot help but be intrigued by the energetic eccentricity which brought such a place into existence and one naturally wonders what sort of a person the builder was. I read letters and documents and listened to recollections handed down the family and a pleasant, interesting character soon emerged. But it was only gradually that I realised that this was not just a rich man's folly but the expression of a serious conviction, a philosophy perhaps although not a religion. As I delved further and learned more of his family and connections, an interesting picture of the different and developing attitudes to the ideas current in the nineteenth century began to emerge.

When one first reads the history of any period one gains, in a way, a false impression because the events, characters and ideas mentioned are the outstanding ones and the people who have the new ideas are ahead of their times. It is what one might call the next rank of people, those who are alert, educated and receptive but not originators, who take up the ideas and spread them. They often modify them in the process by what aspects they accept or reject so that there is always a time-lag between the first expression of an idea and its general currency. I have found it absorbing to try to discover how far the lives of these particular people were affected by the ideas and fashions of their day and which of these appealed particularly to different people according to their different characters.

The central character in what follows must be the Reverend Walter Stevenson Halliday, M.A., born in 1794 the younger son of a Scottish naval surgeon, because he provided the lasting monument and focal point by building the house and founding the Glenthorne estate on the coast of Exmoor. He had no children but his sister, Elizabeth, had married another naval man, Sir William Cosway, secretary to Admiral Lord Collingwood, and it was their son, William Halliday Cosway, who inherited Walter's life's work. This nephew married one Maria Farquhar, youngest daughter of a banker, whose father, Sir Walter Farquhar, had been physician to the Prince Regent. The Farquhars were old friends and compatriots and were already connected by marriage so that we have a close circle of similar people, all upper class and professional, all well enough established to take education and the good things of life for granted, but still, largely owing to good fortune in war, moving confidently a little higher. They were not great but they were never far from those currently considered so. They were not aristocratic but they were undeniably 'in society' and, as most of them were not only intelligent but intellectually inclined, they were interested in the ideas of their time. More particularly, the later journals help us to understand not only how the Exmoor landscape could be seen in a wider perspective but also how the Exmoor scene could become the criterion for testing the worth of landscapes elsewhere.

They were all convinced of the virtue of simplicity, although their ideas of what constituted simplicity varied from generation to generation. One other fact emerged as I read on and that was that the people involved all belonged to a generation of spenders, born with silver spoons in their mouths and enjoying the legacies from previous generations of getters. Even their story is not one

8

of rags to riches because, although they had not been born very rich, they were all educated gentlemen. By their exertions, however, their heirs had considerable means and, being entirely free from money worries, were able seriously to concentrate on self-fulfilment!

THE MONEYMAKERS

Although my present concern is with the spenders, it would perhaps be as well to start with a brief account of the men who actually made the money that went into the building of the house – some would say folly – and founded Glenthorne estate on Exmoor. These were three gentlemen – Dr Simon Halliday, Sir William Cosway Kt and Sir Walter Farquhar, Bart. Their ages varied but they had one thing in common – they all got their chance in the Napoleonic Wars.

Simon Halliday was neither the oldest nor the most distinguished but, as the Reverend Walter Stevenson Halliday was his son, it is convenient to start with him. He was born in 1756 at Whinnyrig near Annan in Dumfriesshire. His family was an old-established and a respected one but, as he was the younger son of a younger son, he had no expectations at all. He studied medicine and then became a naval surgeon for seven years, serving with Earl Howe in America and then as chief medico to Sir Edward Hughes in the East Indies. By 1787, however, he seems to have left the navy for, in that year, he married Elizabeth, only daughter of Dr Thomas Harvie of Jamaica, and settled in London as a medical practitioner and Surgeon Extraordinary to the Duke of Clarence. It seemed that he was in a fair way of becoming a fashionable doctor but this interlude lasted for only two years before his 'private affairs' demanded his presence in India. Presumably he had invested money as he acquired it while he was in the navy with Sir Edward Hughes. There is no account of what this particular business was but he stayed on as an employee of the East India Company, first as Magistrate of Police in the district of Bombay and then, after various other posts, he spent seven years as Naval Superintendent and prize agent to the navy in the port of Bombay. His children, two sons and two daughters, were sent home to England for their education but, by 1807, his health was fragile enough and his fortune robust enough for him and Elizabeth to return to England.

He was by then fifty-one and no longer in the best of health. Moreover, his eldest brother, Robert, had died unmarried some time in the 1790s leaving him the small paternal estate of

10

Whinnyrig but he showed no disposition to settle in Scotland or merely to invest his money safely and live at leisure on the income. He bought some land in Annandale as it became available but he settled in London, renting a house first in Harley Street and then in Upper Berkeley Street, a newly-developed area favoured by nabobs. He became a partner in the banking house of Herries, Farquhar & Co., which had its premises in St James Street, and put some of his money to good use there, but he also became a partner in a brewery business in Ipswich.

On the whole he continued to prosper though perhaps not with the inevitability that seemed to have been his in India. Having decided that the brewery was not perhaps a good investment, he was in the process of extricating himself from the partnership when one partner died. Soon afterwards, the third, who fortunately had only a small share, went bankrupt and fled to France, taking the company books with him. The tidying-up and selling-out was still going on some time after Simon's death!

There was another tiresome complication at the bank in 1823. At intervals since 1810, Simon had lent money at the current rate of five per cent per annum to a relation by marriage of one of the partners, who was himself a relation by marriage of Simon's. The security was a Jamaican plantation called Castle Wemyss. In 1823 the loan had reached £23,000 and there was no possibility of repayment of the principal or payment of the interest, so the estate of 1117 acres and 200 slaves was handed over to Simon.

He had no intention of making the two months' voyage to inspect his new property: he had had enough of travel and hot climates and he could not spare the time from his other affairs, so he ran it through an agent but, since England had by now lost the sugar monopoly, it was no longer easy to make a fortune from the West Indies. The detailed reports of the daily running of the estate still exist, together with the bills and receipts for goods despatched and sugar and rum received, neatly tied in bundles with faded pink tape. They make fascinating reading now but, in one letter, Simon says he wishes he had never heard of the West Indies. It was to prove even more of a worry and a loss to his heir when he owned it, willy-nilly, through all the unrest and embarrassment of abolition.

There were family difficulties too. His daughter, Elizabeth, was satisfactorily married to Sir William Cosway, a young man whose character and outlook pleased and reassured him even though his fortune did not quite match Simon's own. His younger daughter, Anne, however, had made a less satisfactory marriage. Her husband, William Gracie Johnstone, was described first as a merchant in London and later as a banker in Florence, but at one point he lived in Florence because, as an undischarged bankrupt, he could not return to England. It seemed, too, that, although Johnstone was a fellow countryman and some sort of connection, Simon had never quite trusted him. Although Elizabeth's marriage portion had all been handed over to her husband, Anne's was put in trust for her children and her husband could use only the income! She had five children in quick succession and then died. One of her sons and her two daughters died in their youth soon after Simon.

The greatest sorrow, however, was the death of his eldest son, George, in 1823. Both boys, George and Walter, had been educated at Eton and Exeter College, Oxford but, while George followed his father into banking, Walter, as was often the case with younger sons, was put to the Church. George seems to have been a satisfactory son and so the loss must have been great when, in Cologne, he caught a fever and died. Walter may well have been loved as much as George but he was certainly not trusted in the same way for he had frivolous ideas about the Romantic and Picturesque and was known to be lukewarm about business. There was comfort, however, to be derived from Elizabeth' satisfactory husband, William Cosway, so Simon did what he could just before he died by making William one of the executors of his will. In this way he hoped that he had safeguarded what was still a handsome fortune, calculated at his death at something like £161,000.

Born in 1783, William Richard Cosway was only eleven years older than Walter Halliday, but Simon seems to have looked on him as a near-contemporary and trusted his sobriety and sense in a way that he obviously did not trust Walter's. It was probable that, as William had been old enough to serve in the navy in the late wars, he was considered as one of the brotherhood, but he also had the advantage in Simon's eyes of having learned the value of money by earning his own fortune.

There is remarkably little information among the masses of family papers about Cosway's early life but, according to an obituary in the *Gentleman's Magazine*, his father was a baker in Devonport. Perhaps snobbish descendants preferred to forget this! There seem to have been a number of Cosways in the West Country and one of them certainly achieved fame bordering on notoriety: that one was William's uncle, Richard Cosway, the miniaturist, whose life, according to one biographer, was 'full of colour and effect'. Others, however, of more sober outlook, seem to have been connected with the navy so it was perhaps not surprising that William was first employed in the victualling office in the dockyard. He then went into the navy as a captain's secretary and later as a purser before finally becoming Admiral Lord Collingwood's trusted secretary. At the battle of Trafalgar only Lord Collingwood, Cosway and Captain Rotherham were left alive on the poop and quarter-deck of the *Royal Sovereign*. The *Gentleman's Magazine* adds that Cosway was severely wounded in the head. At all events, he finally left the navy with a good name and a reasonable fortune, although a smaller one than many others acquired in the war.

Here the story diverges. According to one account, he wanted to marry one of Collingwood's daughters, but Collingwood was by now dead and the trustees did not consider him wealthy or well-connected enough and rejected him. The *Gentleman's Magazine* has a more flattering and romantic version. According to the same obituary, Collingwood

> expressed a wish that his daughter should marry him. The young lady was not unwilling and everything was arranged for the completion of this auspicious and highly flattering union when Sir William had the misfortune to have both his legs broken as he was driving through Temple Bar in a gig. This calamity compelled him to confine hmself to his chamber for some years; the young lady had constancy enough to wait no less than three years for his recovery but, that being still regarded as doubtful, she married another. In a very few weeks afterwards, however, Mr Cosway's recovery was pronounced complete and he, too, married the lady who is still living to lament his loss.

Whichever version is correct, it is certainly true that in his will he left £100 to Sarah Collingwood and the same to the two children of Patience Collingwood, but he does not seem to have been unhappy in his marriage with Simon Halliday's daughter, Elizabeth, and he made good use of her dowry of £15,000.

Although his family was Devonian, he settled at Bilsington near Ashford in Kent for carefully thought-out reasons. He claimed that ' ..... it is always most advantageous for a permanent investment to select the County (if there be a choice) where wages are highest for the rent is, after all, what remains after every charge of cultivation etc. is deducted and labour is the great charge; it would follow accordingly to my views that where the greatest deduction is made for that item the rest is likely to be most permanent for, with daily improving communications, there will not long exist a great difference between prices in this or that County. In Kent wages are higher than any part of England – our lowest wages are 12/- per week and ranging up to 15/-.'

In 1825, having made his choice, he invested his own and his wife's money in the Bilsington estate and then, after Simon's death, his children's legacies were put to the same use. Walter did not think this was quite the thing but when, after a good deal of wrangling, William secured a legacy for the child born some time *after* Simon's death, Walter was outraged. William might consider Walter unbusinesslike but Walter considered William too sharp by half. In fact, William never seemed to feel he had enough money to be quite comfortable in his busy public life.

He hoped to become a member of Parliament but, meanwhile, he was a very active magistrate during the agricultural troubles and was knighted in 1829 for his bravery in quelling a riot which had been ugly enough to make it necessary for him formally to read the Riot Act. He was not, however, a hard or mean man and seems to have wanted money not for self-aggrandisement but to put his ideas into practice and, for his time, he was very sympathetic to the plight of the agricultural labourer. Even at the height of the unrest, he wrote in a letter to a friend: 'I am surrounded with business and all sorts of devilments – being in the saddle as the active Magistrate of the district you may suppose I have scarcely an hour to myself – one or two more decisive checks will put an end to intimidation (with an increase of wages!) – we perceive already a reasonableness in the tone of the demand which did not exist before.' In 1830 he lent £150 for four poor families to emigrate to America and was remembered for some time as an excellent landlord, much concerned about rural poverty and interested in the Reform Bill.

Temperamentally, he enjoyed managing money and affairs and, in spite of his complaints of being pressed by business, he worked hard to carry out the terms of Simon's will. It was, however, tantalising and at times infuriating to be associated with someone who seemed to him as impossible as Walter. While William was working hard to stretch his fortune as far as possible for the founding of a family and the improvement of a community, Walter had used a part of his large inheritance to start building a romantic house in a near-inaccessible combe on Exmoor and had then married a penniless orphan of mature years and disappeared on a protracted honeymoon, first to Rome and then to 'an old tower in the Jura converted into a comfortable abode'.

To William, pressed for time and money and trying to cope with insurrection caused by misery, it must have been particularly exasperating to correspond with someone who was first in Rome 'feasting amid the ruins and recollections of the glory and splendour of former days' and then in the Alps, leading a life 'so retired and tranquil ... that we can furnish no materials for a letter'. When not admiring the scenery, Walter was apparently immersed in Gibbon's library which he had bought on the way to his tower.

There was, however, another more solid reason why William found Walter's behaviour so disquieting. Simon had willed that, failing direct male heirs, his property should go first to his eldest nephew, Simon Halliday Johnstone, who was Anne's son, and, failing him, to William's son, William Halliday Cosway. As Walter's new wife was over forty when they married, and there was no immediate sign of a child, there seemed little chance of a direct heir and, as Anne's son was delicate, there seemed every prospect that William was working for his own son. If only Walter could be persuaded to buy good land in Kent, preferably not too far from Bilsington, young William might one day be one of the most influential men in that county. It was a possibility worth fighting for.

It seemed that, with care and good management, he could not fail to establish his family in a far more prosperous way than his forebears. He had failed, so far, to get into Parliament, but he was pulling his land into shape and spending an increasingly busy public life, not only as a magistrate, but as a member of various boards. He seems, however, to have been more prone to accident on land than at sea. In June 1834, he was on his way home by coach from a meeting in London when the horses were startled by something, shied, and bolted and the coach overturned. Sir

William was travelling on the box but, when the commotion started, he tried to climb over the roof to safety and was thrown from the coach with such violence that, according to a contemporary newspaper account, his brains burst out of his ears. He was carried to an inn where he was found, not unnaturally, to be dead.

He was only fifty-one, and he left his wife, weak from a recent miscarriage, with five young children. As one would have expected his affairs were in order but, as his estate was still a fairly recent acquisition, it needed his particular care and interest. He was indeed cut off in his prime after surviving all the dangers of war at sea.

There appear to have been many people beside his wife who sincerely regretted his death. In Bilsington, on the crest of a slight hill, in the middle of a field, stands an obelisk, 52 feet high, inscribed:

As a Tribute of Respect
to the memory of
Sir William Richard Cosway
This monument was erected by
his friends
and
The Reformers of East Kent
In the year MDCCCXXXV

It has obviously since become an embarrassment to the small village. It was repaired in 1893 and 1948 and, at present, is in a rather ruinous state after being struck by lightning in 1967. When it finally crumbles, it may yet be remembered, for the garage opposite is called 'Monument Garage'. There is another memorial which would have been to his taste; the village council houses are called Cosway Cottages. Elizabeth retired with her family to the pretty Regency villa at Cowes which Simon had built just before his death and had left to her. By way of a change, she and the children spent a good deal of time on Exmoor with Walter while Bilsington was managed until her son came of age.

The third member of the money-making trio was, in fact, the oldest and most notable but, as his family's closest involvement with Glenthorne comes later, he comes last in the present narrative. Walter Farquhar, later to become a baronet, was born in 1738 of a family very similar to Simon Halliday's. His father, the Reverend Robert Farquhar, was Minister of Garloch. An earlier Robert had been Provost of Aberdeen in 1646. Walter was educated in Aberdeen and took his M.A. before going on to study medicine at Aberdeen, Edinburgh and Glasgow, but abandoned his studies without graduating and joined the Army Medical Service. Like Simon Halliday, he served under Lord Howe but, as he was eighteen years older, at an earlier time. While he was stationed with his regiment at Gibraltar, he either became bored or ambition must have stirred again, for he obtained leave of absence and spent nearly a year and a half attending hospitals in Paris and Rouen amongst others. In due course, on a plea of ill health, he left the army and settled in London as a medical practitioner. 1796 seemed to be his year of achievement for he obtained the degree of M.D. from Aberdeen; was admitted Fellow of the College of Physicians at Edinburgh; became a Licentiate of the College of Physicians in London; and was made a baronet.

From then on he was increasingly in demand as a fashionable physician. His patients were almost all of rank, influence – and wealth – and included William Pitt, but his most distinguished patron was the Prince of Wales to whom he became physician in ordinary. In the *Dictionary of National Biography* it is recorded that 'Farquhar was considered a very able and successful physician, while his high personal character won him many friends, but he is not known to have made any contribution to medical science or literature.' Presumably, he was kept too busy with his patients to have time for research and, even if one suspects that his greatest asset was a good bedside manner, after all, at that time of comparatively small medical knowledge, that was probably even more important than now! Even though he did not contribute to medical knowledge, his grateful patients contributed largely to his fortune and, by 1813, six years before his death, he was able to cut his practice down considerably and to spend more time at his Surrey home, Polesden Lacy, which he had bought from the playwright, Sheridan. Then it was not the vast house which the National Trust now preserves so beautifully; it was a relatively modest Regency villa, but still undeniably a handsome gentleman's residence and then, as now, set in most beautiful grounds.

It is not certain whether the Farquhars and Hallidays knew each other originally in Scotland but they became related by marriage when, in 1771, Walter Farquhar married Anne Harvie, a widow with one daughter, and in 1787 Simon Halliday married the daughter. Walter's and Anne's eldest son, Thomas, became a banker and was in fact the 'Farquhar' of Herries, Farquhar & Co., the bank in which Simon became a partner in 1807. Thus the families became closely connected by marriage and business. Through the Hallidays, the Farquhars must have known the Cosways and, in the next generation, Thomas' youngest daughter, Maria, married Walter Halliday's nephew, William Cosway, thus completing the circle and eventually becoming Glenthorne's second mistress.

CREATING A LEGEND

Inspiration

Most people will be familiar with the habit families have of endowing their members with characters which are subsequently never modified however the subjects change or develop. To the practical, busy Hallidays, Farquhars and Cosways, Simon Halliday's second son, Walter, was, when a boy, an unbusiness-like romantic, rather like William Beckford and Mackenzie's *Man of Feeling* rolled into one. It was felt that there was a lurking extravagance and irresponsibility in his make-up which needed watching. While he was a younger son, the situation was not too serious, for his love of books made the Church a natural profession for him, and his tendency to extravagance of idea and expression, while not leading him into the excesses of Methodism, made him a good preacher in the not too onerous curacies which he held under useful relations and connections. When his sober, responsible brother, George, died, however, there was a good deal of disquietude felt in the family.

As ever, there was some foundation for family misgivings. In spite of friends, relations and connections busy all over the world, Walter never seems to have shown any desire to go into business, although he travelled and visited exhaustively and, as soon as he had any money at all, showed a marked disposition to enjoy it and make it work for him rather than be forced to work at increasing it. It was true, too, that in some ways he was a follower of the new Romantic school of thought: he read the modern poets, Wordsworth, Shelley, Keats and Coleridge; he read modern Gothic novels too but, more than this, he subscribed to the new aesthetic school of the Picturesque, despising the smooth, regular beauty of an ordered landscape, and admiring the rough, irregular and natural, condemning the neo-classical in building as a sterile import and seeking to promote a return to an indigenous architecture based on the Elizabethan and Jacobean. Worst of all, he followed his interests with exhausting enthusiasm.

Obviously, these were disturbing traits in one who would, before long, have the management of large sums of hard-earned money but, in other respects, he was reassuringly normal by the standards of his time and class. In appearance, this thirty-five year old clergyman was far from the Byronic figure one begins to imagine. He was a stocky man, broad in the shoulders and a trifle short in the legs. He had a big head and, when allowance is made for the portraitists' best efforts, he was not particularly handsome, though his face was pleasant, his eyes bright and his long mouth curled a little at the corners. In his youth he seems to have been known as a good preacher but, although he was a seriously religious man, this religion was of the comfortable, kindly, broad variety and he would certainly have approved his old friend Admiral Fairfax Moresby's statement of belief: 'I was born in the Church of England, and I mean to die in the Church of England and there is my prayer-book, Sir. I have loyally served my God and my King for more than half a century and I should like to know what more there is to be said about the matter, Sir.'

In politics he started off a Tory and stayed in that persuasion. He was, in fact, much more conservative than his reforming brother-in-law, Sir William Cosway, and those he employed on his wild aesthetic ideas were expected to work diligently for no more than the going rate. He seems to have had little or no interest in general reform, being content to keep to the old paternalistic idea of help and reward to those he personally knew to be deserving. When it came to the business of acquisition he was sharp enough to know when people were intending to cheat or overcharge him, but realistic enough to attempt to work out how much his desires were worth to him, and kindly enough not to be too rigorous in 'correcting' those of whom he disapproved. In fact, his dangerous new ideas were at least limited to the aesthetic. He quite obviously had all his father's vigour and imagination but he was bent on enjoying life in a way which Simon had been unable to afford until, presumably, it was too late. He was obviously not nearly as alarming a character as his elders made out although, as things turned out, a good many of their forebodings were justified.

After his brother's death, but before his father's, Walter must have been provided with a substantial income because, while Simon was building a Regency villa in Cowes overlooking the Solent, Walter was acquiring a good deal of property in the little fishing village of Lynmouth and building his own romantic villa halfway up the cliff behind it, looking out over the Bristol Channel. No one seems to know why he chose this part of the country, except that he had visited a friend in North Devon and found that it provided just the wild rugged landscape he most admired. There was certainly some literary precedent, for Coleridge had written *Kubla Khan* in an Exmoor farmhouse a few miles up the coast, and Shelley had stayed, very briefly, in Lynmouth with his first wife.

Walter was enjoying himself but his father must have been disquieted because, when he realised the serious nature of what was, in fact, his terminal illness, he hastily revised his will. In his first will, after various bequests, he had left everything unreservedly to George but, in his second, he took steps to preserve his hard-won fortune. In one memorandum for the drawing-up of this new will, he restated his previous bequests, and then went on to say: 'Whatever may remain after this, I wish to be invested either in land or Government securities, so that my son, Walter, cannot inter-meddle with anything but the interest, which I mean he should receive during his life.' And, in another, he starts off by saying: 'I wish to leave my son, W.S. Halliday, £30,000 for his sole use and benefit but, having worked very hard all my life and wishing my name to be handed down to posterity, I therefore will the remainder to be disposed of as follows...' and then he restates his intentions. He was a just but careful man.

There is no suggestion that Walter was hurt by the terms of his father's will. Gradually, he was to find his conscientious co-executor, Sir William, an irritation but, meanwhile, there was not much to grumble about. After all, apart from £30,000 for present use, he had the income from the small Scottish estate and from the West Indian one which was not, at that time, the liability it was later to become. Then there was the income from the residue of the estate, which turned out to be at least £70,000. The prospects were pleasing, and he set about enlarging his ideas.

At about this time, a piece of land on the Exmoor coast, nearer to the Somerset boundary than Lynmouth, came up for sale and, sitting on a flat stone halfway down the steepest seaward combe on this piece, he decided that he must have it and build a house on the cliff edge at the bottom of the combe. The land was bought, the Lynmouth property was gradually disposed of, and building began, starting with a winding drive more than 2½ miles long. The stone on which he sat, still to be found if you search carefully, was inscribed with his initials and the date and was known thereafter as 'The Decision Stone'. The laborious creation of a legend had begun!

The agricultural land was, and still is, high, poor, and windswept, but the cliffs were, and still are, spectacular. There are deep, tortuous combes and thick natural oak woods which run right down to the sea. Their luxuriance contrasts sharply with the barren sweep of the heather moor at the top of the cliffs and the rocky beach at the bottom, with caves and twisted strata, where the trees thin out on the more precipitous cliffs. Even now, when North Devon is a popular place for tourists, people look insignificant in this landscape. In 1829 nature must have seemed alarmingly paramount. There is even very little history evident in these parts of the sort that gives some human comfort. The farms on the coastal strip are, in fact, very old, some mentioned in the Doomsday Book, and almost all in existence in the fourteenth century but, in the early nineteenth century, they were as small and poor as they had ever been, with little high-banked fields, and their livelihood drawn mainly from sheep rough-grazed on the moor.

There is evidence all over of pre-history in barrows and standing-stones. At the top of Glenthorne drive is Old Burrow, a Roman look-out post which must have made any Roman stationed there extremely miserable from exposure to cold and wet. At the top of Countisbury Hill is Wind Hill, a prehistoric hill fort where the local tribesmen are said to have repulsed a Viking attack, though why the Vikings were stupid enough to attempt scaling such formidable cliffs is difficult to understand. In the early nineteenth century a good deal of local energy and enterprise went into smuggling. Even here, although danger from pursuit must have been less than on the south coast, danger from the sea must have been a good deal greater, for the currents are bad and the little bays rocky.

At the bottom of the biggest combe, near the county boundary, 700 feet below the hill top and only 100 feet above the sea, there were two little meadows. They were far away from the nearest farm or other pasture, and their main use was said to be to smugglers. A few sheep in them could give a reason for being there at all and their feet could obliterate the pack-ponies' hoofmarks. The cove below was as navigable as most on the coast; there were one or two caves large enough for temporary storage and it was possible to make one's way up on either side of the county boundary. It was on a flat stretch beside these fields that Walter, tiresomely for local trade, decided to build his commodious modern manor house.

The site he chose must be one of the most spectacular in England. It must also be one of the most impractical and inconvenient and, here already, is the central paradox of the whole enterprise: the reconciling of the apparently unreconcilable which begins with the tremendous effort of making a civilised oasis in the middle of the most difficult and uncivilised place so that sophisticated and educated people could live in it and appreciate the unsophisticated and wild. It is easy enough to understand the growing feeling that as civilisation increases one should not lose touch with the natural world. This feeling, which began about the time of the French Revolution, is with us so much more strongly now as towns go on growing but, practically, it is very difficult to tread the untrodden ways without leaving any footprints, particularly if one wants to do it in tolerable comfort.

It took most of a year to construct a drive down the combe to the proposed building site; it is nearly three miles long and drops the necessary 700 feet in easy stages but with a number of spectacular sweeping curves and tight corners. However, when one does arrive, one recognises the beautifully sheltered nature of the site, so well protected by the hills from the prevailing south west wind that many delicate plants flourish.

One's immediate reaction to the house is 'how romantic' – whatever one subsequently decides one means by that. Built of pinkish-grey local stone, its complicated mass of ridges and ornamental chimneys seem to rise in all directions, making it look far larger than it is. It backs up against the high hill so that, if you crane your neck and look up through the back windows, you see the roots of trees on a level with the roofs, but the big front windows and the terrace look straight over thirteen miles of sea to the cliffs and mountains of Wales. On both sides of the house, the trees slide down the hills to reddish cliffs and, on clear nights, the Nash Light shines on the walls and the moon shines over the sea through the branches of an old pine tree. It has inspired countless poems, some of them very bad, but in winter the sun never rises high enough to shine over the hills and down to the house and, although undeniably grand and very beautiful, it can then be extremely gloomy.

The Latest Ideas

Professor Pevsner, in his County guides, calls the house 'an undistinguished building in a striking position'. This is, in a way, a tribute to its creator, for he was a devoted follower of the cult of the Picturesque as expounded by Uvedale Price, and a good deal of his inspiration for the building came from P.F. Robinson's *Rural Architecture*, a very popular book which must have been a sort of *Daily Mail Book of House Plans* in its time. Both of these writers stress the importance of fitting one's building to the landscape, and Robinson believed that Georgian classical architecture was a sterile aberration from tradition which should be abandoned along with the highly organised 'natural landscape' of Capability Brown. Glenthorne was not conceived as a rich man's folly, but as a serious attempt to carry out these ideals and, while many people were still Gothicising their classical exteriors and redesigning their parks, Walter was in the fortunate position of being able to choose his landscape and fit his house into it. He felt sure enough of his ideas not to feel the need of a fashionable architect, and he followed the more usual practice of his day in merely consulting with the builder and employing a Clerk of Works. This led to a little confusion in places, particularly in the arrangements for letting in light to odd passages, but the result is individual and speaks loudly of its creator.

Uvedale Price's *Essay on the Picturesque* and his *Dialogue on the Distinct Character of the Picturesque and Beautiful* are still in the Glenthorne library, together with Robinson's *Rural Architecture* annotated in Walter's handwriting. Together, these books form an important key to the philosophy behind the romantic idea of landscape and the Gothic and Tudor revival. It is interesting to note in passing that Walter's 'new editions' of Uvedale Price are dated 1796 and 1801 and, although his 'Robinson' is dated 1828, it is the third edition. It was 1829 before Walter started putting these ideas into practice, and the result was still considered by many to be uncomfortably modern while, only fifteen miles away, and seven years earlier, a new house was being put up at Arlington, traditionally square, white, and porticoed with pastoral parkland and a ha-ha.

Burke's definition of the sublime and beautiful had been much discussed, and seems to have been universally accepted, but Price is the champion of the 'Picturesque' which he claims is 'much less obvious, less generally attractive (than the really sublime or beautiful) and has been totally neglected by professed improvers.' He spends a great deal of time discussing what the Picturesque is, but concludes briefly that: 'picturesqueness appears to hold a station between beauty and sublimity; and on that account, perhaps, is more happily blended with them both than they are with each other.' Practically speaking, he has had enough of the smooth symmetry of the neo-classical buildings and the carefully controlled and contrived landscapes of Kent, Brown and Repton, which went with them. He feels the need of something with more vigour, but realises that the sublime, with the sensations of awe and terror which it arouses, cannot easily be found or lived with! 'Upon the whole,' he says, 'it seems to me, that as intricacy in the disposition, and variety in the forms, the tints and lights and the shadows of objects are the great objects of picturesque scenery, so monotony and boldness are the great defects of improved places.' Presumably Jane Austen had the same idea in mind when she satirised the improver in Mansfield Park. Naturally, neither she nor Price could foresee that natural growth and a lack of gardeners have, in time, made Mr Brown's efforts picturesque enough for us.

Uvedale Price was outspokenly rude about Capability Brown but he, in his turn, suffered equally from detractors who labelled him as the man who sought to put the cart before the horse by designing the landscape to look like pictures. In fact, his idea was ingenious: he held that we should help our imaginations by trying to analyse what gives us pleasure in great landscape paintings and then to use the same principles in planning our buildings and landscapes. 'With respect to the art of improving,' he writes, 'we may look upon pictures as a set of experiments of the different ways in which trees, buildings, water, etc., may be disposed, grouped, and accompanied in the most beautiful and striking manner and in every style, from the most simple and rural to the grandest and most ornamental.' One has only to look at a few of Price's preferred pictures, mostly by Claude, Poussin and Salvator Rosa, to see what a happy hunting ground he gave to both detractors and over-enthusiastic admirers, and why Walter's relations were so disquieted! Detractors enjoyed themselves demanding whether they were expected to live in ruins, wear exiguous clothes, sandals and funny hats while playing rustic pipes or asking, with some reason, what happened to the carefully contrived effect when one changed one's vantage point. The enthusiasts made instant ruins and did their utmost to preserve any tumbledown cottages or blasted oaks.

Despite this, however, Price's basic idea, that of studying natural beauty, of treating it with sensibility, and of doing our best to fit our buildings into it, leaving any violence to nature itself, is the cardinal rule of planners and improvers today. His practical suggestions, too, are for the most part those which we still hold to be very good. He talks of the importance of roofs and chimneys, and the need for variety in them, but he also says: 'But whatever changes and improvements be made ... in general the common materials of the country and the common methods of using them will, of course, be employed; and such uniformity and plainness are not only natural and proper, but give a zest to any deviations from them ... '

The basic definition that smoothness equals beauty and roughness equals the picturesque is an intellectual distinction. A sentimental distinction comes in when one considers the nature of things that exhibit roughness: old hovels, old houses, old women, and the way of life that would seem to be necessary to produce a plentiful supply of these interesting objects. Jane Austen describes the situation in *Sense and Sensibility* in a conversation between Edward and Marianne on the subject of landscape. Edward approves of the landscape around Barton, although not for the same reasons as Marianne:

> It exactly answers my idea of a fine country, because it unites beauty with utility – and I daresay it is picturesque too, because you admire it; I can easily believe it to be full of rocks and promontories, grey moss and brushwood, but these are all lost to me. I know nothing of the picturesque ... I like a fine prospect, but not on picturesque principles. I do not like crooked, twisted, blasted trees. I admire them much more if they are tall, straight and flourishing. I do not like ruined, tattered cottages. I am not fond of nettles or thistles, or heath blossoms. I have more pleasure in a snug farmhouse than a watch-tower – and a troop of tidy, happy villagers please me better than the finest banditti in the world.

Marianne, we are told, looked in amazement at Edward.

This does, in fact, neatly state a dilemma that was to grow in the

26

progressive, inventive nineteenth century, and exercises us now to such an extent that we feel we must make laws to deal with it. How does one reconcile worship of the natural, the rugged and the old with progress, prosperity and work for all? Price is obviously aware that he has a problem in reconciling his love of the picturesque with his feelings of social benevolence and, after lengthy discussion, he concludes that: 'The fact is that neatness and regularity are so connected with the habitation of man, that they almost always please on a small scale, and where the connection is immediate: especially when they are contrasted with what is wild and luxuriant without being slovenly.' To us he seems to get unduly agitated about trying to explain such things as why he is not betraying his principles in admiring well-trained fruit trees as well as blasted oaks but, on the whole, his ideals and problems are ours. We talk and write endlessly about the need to interfere with the natural landscape as little as possible and to fit our buildings into their environment while we assume the importance of high living standards. We, too, believe in working to promote the comfort and enjoyment of the inhabitants, although most of the female part of the population would not agree with Price that 'the most delightful image of peace and security is that of women doing their washing at the stream.'

Walter Halliday found himself the perfect picturesque site, but it was only later that the difficulties of promoting comfort there began to appear. If Price was Walter's general guide, P.F. Robinson, Architect F.A.S., provided a number of his practical ideas and some of his buildings appear to have come straight from *Rural Architecture, being a series of Designs for Ornamental Cottages* first published in 1822. Robinson does not discuss the landscape; his book is solely concerned with architectural design that does not argue with its setting. In one important way he disagrees with Price for, in his conclusion, Price advocates taking the best from all ages and countries while Robinson categorically states that his aim is to restore a species of architecture 'till now sadly neglected and almost forgotten'. He does, however, agree completely with Price on two points: local methods and materials should be used as far as ever possible and social benefit is of the highest importance. His book has designs for all sorts and sizes of buildings needed on an estate from a boat-house through every degree of estate worker's house to a parsonage, a 'residence' and a court of 34 almshouses with a chapel.

The prevailing style of Robinson's design can probably best be described as Jacobean-ish. Windows are latticed, and surmounted by hood moulds, chimneys are massive, generally grouped together and highly ornamented. Gables with ornamental barge-boards are everywhere, sometimes with finials and pendants as well. A large number of houses have porches supported by 'rude oak posts' up which creepers are expected to climb. Thatch and oak shingles are often shown on the roofs. From the point of view of both fitness and cheapness, Robinson strongly advocates the use of local materials and local labour. In the preface to his design for a gamekeeper's cottage (one storey, containing kitchen, parlour and outhouse) he writes:

> As it is the Author's wish to prove in the course of the present work that the humblest dwelling may be erected, by a proper management of materials, so as to produce a pleasing effect, and at the same expense as the commonplace and ill-shaped structures now so invariably seen in all parts of the country, he purposes giving designs of the simplest form and construction, thence gradually rising to those of more consequence. In the choice of materials, the rudest should be best adapted to the means of the cottager. Thus unhewn stones, shaped only at the angles with a sparing hand; pebble fronts, or roughcast, may be properly applied, with oak, formed and fitted to its place by the axe alone. The mere woodman is the best artificer for the cottage, and thus expense in wages is saved. External painting should be made to resemble oak, and no other colour used.

The design for the bailiff's house is naturally for a more important structure. It is larger and more highly ornamented, but still designed to be made locally. Robinson explains:

> Although some ornament is applied externally, the whole may be formed by the hand of the labourer with a little instruction. The awning is covered with slit-oak shingles, the ends being rounded with the saw, and a mould being previously cut, the workman quickly produces an effect which is very pleasing. An objection may probably be raised to the ornamental shafted chimney, and it is

true that this creates some labour, but a little
practice will conquer any difficulty which may at
first appear, and the effect will amply pay for this
additional labour. Bricks formed in moulds to
different patterns are easily applied to circular and
octagonal shafts.

There is that sprightly air of refusing to admit difficulties which is
still to be found in do-it-yourself manuals, and which has left so
many of us bitterly undeceived. One wonders if the final results
justified all the rows which must have blown up among these
simple woodmen and rude labourers, but there is still evidence of
much skilful work round Glenthorne. It has, however, been
noticed that, with time, ornamental bricks have a way of
detaching themselves from chimneys and suddenly turning into
garden ornaments. It is interesting to note that, where detail is
concerned, Robinson not only gives scale drawings but quotes
examples: doors and shutters from Iffley Church; ornamental
chimneys from St Cross, Winchester, and Hampton Court. If
Price's ideas held the beginnings of eclecticism, Robinson's held
those of reproduction. Meanwhile, Walter Halliday's ideas might
best be described as inspirational.

As one looks through the plates of *Rural Architecture*, simplicity is
not the word that springs to mind. Indeed, there is often an air of
coy fussiness about these ornamental cottages that reminds one
rather of Walt Disney Tyrolean, but the social idea behind it is one
of simple living. The designs embody a philosophical idea, an
attempt at imaginative kindliness in trying to envisage the needs
and arrange the comforts of the 'people of modest means' who
were to live in them and to create a harmonious whole with
nature. If one wishes to see 'Robinson building' on a large and
successful scale, one has only to go a short distance from
Glenthorne to Selworthy, where Sir Thomas Dyke Acland built a
noteworthy estate village round a green. Sightseers started to
come as the first cottages went up and now, maintained by the
National Trust, the village draws people in their thousands, not
only because it delights and amuses the eye, but because it seems
to embody a vision of peaceful unsophisticated rustic life and
they can indulge for a while in the rural dream. There must
always have been a certain amount of make-believe involved, but
it is successful, and the cottages are good as well as pretty.

Ideas Into Practice

Armed, then, with his ideas and his manuals and having chosen his ideal site, what did Walter manage to create? A good deal of the first year had to be spent in making a drive in order to reach the site and, without mechanical aid, it was something of a feat to cut a track down the combe with an easy enough gradient for horses and carriages. As the crow flies, the house is under two miles from the main road, but the drive is nearly three miles long, and still has a few uncomfortably tight corners. After that, stables had to be built on the site of what was to become the home farm to house the working horses, and then a track to the sea was cut and a landing stage made for materials to come in by sea. Only then could work on the house begin. It was, in fact, built in stages as the need seemed to arise and successive engravings and amateur sketches show its progress from neat villa to spreading manor-house, although it was built all in the same style. Obedient to his ideals, Walter used locally quarried stone which has pink, green, and occasional red streaks in its basic grey. It is put together with ridged cement, which is pink from the local sand used and it is roofed with large Cornish slates. The work was done by a local builder, supervised by a Clerk of the Works from Nynehead, near Wellington.

For all his convictions, however, it seems that Walter could not quite get away from impressions that he had absorbed as he grew up and the house is as much Georgian, mildly Gothicised, as Tudoresque. It has ridged roofs and gables in profusion surmounted, except where change and decay have taken a hand, with carved stone finials and occasional almost pagoda-like turrets. Its shape is far from regular, and there are groups of Tudoresque ornamental chimneys. These were not made by local men but were brought by road from London as far as Porlock, and then by sea to avoid the one-in-four gradient of Porlock Hill. The windows, too, are far from Georgian: some have wide bays, and the flat ones have stone hood-moulds. They are all casements, set in stone mullions, and are Gothicised by glazing-bars set across the corners to make awkward little triangular panes. Some of the bars are wooden and some of cast iron. Over the heavy oak front door, with its flat Tudor arch, is an oriel window with stone bosses underneath, and the attic windows are glazed slits which look defensive, and let far too little light and air into the servants' bedrooms. Despite all this, however, there is a Georgian air about the place, something to do with the proportions of the building, and the fact that it is finished with a Bath stone plinth and string courses along low parapets give it a contained 'lined-up' air. There are no carved barge-boards or rude oak posts, as they were more suitable for cottages, and Walter was certain, right from the start, that he was building a considerable house, and not an overblown cottage.

Inside, there is the same slight confusion of ideas. The rooms are devoid of any nooks and crannies and, although the ceiling height is a little lower than in the grander Georgian houses, there is a feeling for pleasant, airy proportion. The ceiling mouldings are elegantly restrained but, where there is panelling, it is oak, or pine stained to look like oak, and the doors are oak, with Gothic arched panels and ornamental spandrels. The front stairs are also oak but, instead of rising in a massive square well, they ascend in a gentle curve to a white and gold arched landing and are lit from above by an oval skylight, classically proportioned but glazed in rather lurid stained glass of the sort that was to be seen later in the staircase windows of many Victorian suburban villas. The banisters are mahogany with 'barley sugar' turned rails, but they appear to be a later alteration and, judging by the marks on the stair-ends, the original ones were delicately straight and slim. In contrast, the back stairs are massive, and as black as stain can make them. They are cased in panelling collected from various sources and the broad handrail is supported by almost grotesquely heavy turned posts. The cellar stairs descend under this staircase and over the door is fixed a wooden arm, holding a sponge, almost certainly from a ship. There are similar touches to be found all over the estate: ominous signs of unsteadiness in the eyes of the family, no doubt, but looked at from a distance of time they underline a certain lightheartedness which kept on appearing.

The fireplaces are divided in style between the old and the new. The library and billiard room, admittedly the most recent additions, have massive carved oak surrounds, locally made, although the figures on them are so startlingly pagan that they look almost as though they originated somewhere in the jungle rather than on Exmoor in the nineteenth century. There are similar pieces all over the moor where the woodcarving tradition was very strong. They give some idea, not only of the long dark days of foul weather that were to be filled in, but also of the old pagan ideas that were still about. Walter's antiquarian taste did not run to cavernous fireplaces and inglenooks: that seems to have belonged to a more recent taste. His fireplaces were tiled, one with what were supposed to be medieval tiles, and the cast iron firebacks were old, but they were furnished with elegant fire-baskets suitable for burning coal. Elsewhere the surrounds were of marble, some with Gothic arches which gave them a slightly ecclesiastical air.

According to the earliest inventories, the furnishing must have presented some startling contrasts. To begin with, there was a certain amount of inherited furniture, some of it Regency inlaid satinwood and some chinoiserie, collected by Simon in his travels, but Walter's own tastes ran to carved oak and 'antiquities'. The dining room was done almost entirely in his taste. The sideboard, serving table and wine coolers, were veneered in bur oak and had Gothic friezes. There were two small bookcases of such Gothic design that a story grew later that they had come from a monastery. Even the dining chairs were carved oak with red leather seats, but their shape was late Georgian and the carving owed more to Grinling Gibbons than to an Elizabethan carpenter. The rest of the furnishing got a little out of hand, for there was an inherited side table of marble, with curved and gilded legs, and the dining table was mahogany, expanding to take extra leaves. The silver and glass, being inherited, was eighteenth century. Walter's other, and probably earlier, enthusiasm, classical antiquity, took over in the decorations. The marble mantel shelf displayed a lamp and a pair of small urns, all said to be Etruscan and, on stands nearby, stood a pair of large, convincingly battered urns, supposed to have been dug up at Herculaneum. After that, avowed reproduction took over. There were two heads of nymphs by Gibson; in one window, a marble Cupid by Kessels, with removable fig leaf, reclined on a plinth, and in the other, a statue of Venus stood, exposing her cold white marble bottom to the Bristol Channel. The setting must have been as heavy as the meals.

Elsewhere in the house there was a superfluous number of carved oak chests and a good few similar cupboards which overwhelmed the more delicate satinwood and mahogany, and here and there are pieces of what can only be described as souvenir furniture. There is a cabinet and table made with wood from the *Royal George*, and a small table incorporating a piece of the *Mary Rose*, a Tudor ship which sank in the Solent, and was located in the last century and then forgotten until very recently.

Pictures, of course, were an essential part of the furnishing of a gentleman's house, and Walter collected in London and on his travels through Europe until there was not quite enough wall space to accommodate them all, particularly as size was no object. Predictably, they were almost all romantic land and sea-scapes. There were three Salvator Rosas, two Rosa da Tivolis, three Poussins, a Vandervelde, a Luny and a Claude, as well as many unremarkable representations of trees and ruins. Altogether, there must have been almost as much wild nature inside the house as out, and the portraits must have been a relief, giving the inhabitants a slight feeling of companionship.

The entrance hall must, in fact, have been a very good preparation for what to expect in the rest of the house. According to the first inventory, it held a set of oak hall chairs (hard and discouraging of long stays) carved with the family crest, an oak table and hat-stand, marble candelabra with bronze lamps, five marble busts, four suits of armour and various 'trophies and weapons'. Later, it was to bristle with antlers, masks and the feet of red deer, but the nearest Walter got to this sort of furnishing was a few cases of stuffed birds on the bedroom landing. It was all a far cry from the carefully organised interior of the Adam brothers, where every least thing was designed to form a harmonious whole and every chair had its exact position. Glenthorne certainly belonged to the 'I know what I like' school of design, but it spoke loudly of its creator's individuality.

There was one entirely modern installation which must have proved an unmixed blessing. Outside there were privies for the staff but, in an angle of the yard, there jutted out a garderobe tower with slit windows and it housed, one above the other, two of the latest water-closets, the plumbing pipes conveniently running down one shaft.

In 1831 the nucleus of the house was finished and a stone plaque, surmounted by a boar's head and inscribed in Latin, was erected over the courtyard door to commemorate the fact. A year before this, however, feeling, no doubt, that he would soon have a suitable home for a bride, Walter took time off to be married.

Katherine Gardiner's family came from Edinburgh, but she seems to have been left an orphan at an early age and was taken to live with the Hallidays. She had relatives and, although most of them had more brains and education than money and many went to seek and find their fortunes in the New World, it seems that she went to the Hallidays because she could be helpful rather than because she was destitute and she never seems to have been in danger of becoming a downtrodden female dependant. It is said that she was engaged to marry George and that Walter took her over with the rest of the inheritance! Whatever the truth of the situation, and however prosaic the arrangement might seem, it was a very good marriage and the couple's affection and respect for each other lasted until Walter's death. Depending on their expectations, other members of the family must have been glad or sorry that there was very little hope of children, but in all other ways it was a very good arrangement. Whenever Katherine is mentioned, she seems to be described as kind; she was also well-educated, practical, a little prosaic and businesslike. She seemed quite prepared to subscribe to the general idea that Walter was unbusinesslike and, right from the start, shared a good deal of administration with him.

Her portrait, drawn in the 1850s by Walter Severn, shows her looking pleasantly, solidly and composedly out at the world.

Consolidation

Prosaic though the marriage might have been, Walter managed, characteristically, to infuse the whole affair with bustle and excitement. They were to be married by a cousin of Katherine's who had a parish near Sandgate and there was a great worry about whether she would be able to move there in time to fulfil the residential requirements before the date fixed for the wedding. The marriage settlements, being in the hands of the lawyers, were considered at length and duly drawn up on an imposing number of skins, but there was another last minute crisis when it was not certain whether Walter could get to Doctors' Commons in time to obtain the licence. Letters went round and round the family, Katherine's sometimes saying that it would be best to communicate direct with her because 'Walter is so unbusinesslike'. In one to their solicitor, she says: 'Mr Halliday will see you on Friday (and will) obtain the licence from

Doctors' Commons on Saturday ... Perhaps (if you have the time to spare) you will have to goodness to accompany Mr Halliday to Doctors' Commons as he is so little a man of business himself ...' Obviously, she had begun to feel that, if she was going to get married, she must take a hand in the affair!

There was a good deal still to be clarified about Simon's will, mainly to do with the Scottish estate as Scots law differed from English, and this became important when the marriage settlements were being considered. Even so, it is difficult to see why two people of mature years whose time was their own, and who had known each other for years, should find getting married so fraught with incipient crises, except that it made it more exciting!

The union was successfully achieved and the couple set off for a protracted honeymoon, their first destination Rome. Walter had to keep in touch with William and his solicitor and there are various business letters existing from this time, generally somewhat explosive and indignant in character, appearing more so, perhaps, for being written in his large, vigorous and rather illegible handwriting. A couple of letters of Katherine's, however, give a little more idea of how they spent their time. Her correspondent was her old and intimate friend, Bessey, who had married a lawyer called Nash Hilliard. It was on the strength of this friendship that Hilliard became Walter's solicitor, a job that must sometimes have been more onerous than expected! Walter and Katherine had been married in May, but it was in December that Katherine was writing from Rome: 'My dear husband is in all his glory in Rome – he is, you know, quite an enthusiast – and is feasting here amid the ruins and recollections of the glory and splendour of former days. We keep apart from English society, of which there is too much here, devoting our mornings to exhibits and sight-seeing – and spending our evenings by our own fireside.'

Walter seems already to have owned the Château des Clées, a converted tower in the Jura, and when they moved on there it seems they spent their time in a similar way. Katherine writes to Bessey: 'Our old tower in the Jura is converted into a comfortable abode and is in the midst of splendid scenery affording ... delightful rambles to those who are equal to climb the mountains, a level walk is unknown in this country ... We live quite retired, a Man and a Maid forms our establishment. Walter's purchase of Gibbon's Library now proves a source of constant gratification to him.'

In theory, the same kind of life awaited them back home at Glenthorne, but in fact there was nearly always the bustle and business of expansion going on there. Perhaps that is why, during the next few years, they retreated to the Continent at fairly frequent intervals, leaving affairs in the hands of solicitors, agents and bailiffs, while they wandered and admired and collected pictures and books.

Before very long, there was another burst of building at Glenthorne. By 1839 the rocky hillside had been excavated so that the house could be extended inland to provide new kitchens and servants' quarters. The new kitchens were spacious and equipped to the highest modern standards. The sinks, lead lined, in the butler's pantry, were placed conveniently under the windows, although these windows looked straight into the hillside. In the back kitchen was a modern closed stove and though the long narrow fire-grate, needed for roasting, in the front kitchen must have roasted the cooks as well as the meat, it was fitted with a most ingenious water-powered spit: a small water-wheel was installed in the thickness of the wall next to the fireplace, water was piped to it and, when the tap was turned on, the water turned the wheel which powered the shaft of the spit. Later, when a new larder was needed, one was dug into the hillside outside the back door. It was floored and shelved with white marble and the slated roof covered with turves which could be watered in hot weather for added coolness. The larder was reached by a covered way and on the roof of this passage was perched the meat safe. The meat hung conveniently in a draught, but could be reached only by a ladder, and it must have needed an operation involving at least two people to lift down the huge pieces of meat that were regularly consumed. The new servants' hall was made impressive by the black oak carved staircase and by a massive oak table and bench made to fit exactly along one wall. One end is carved with the house's name and on the other is the family crest of a boar's head and the date, 1839. The top is made from five planks, each nearly twelve feet long. It seemed that Walter followed the plan, still popular, of having the latest conveniences in the kitchen and antiques in the rest of the house, nor was he averse to making his own antiques!

Another extension was probably to give pleasure to the house's new mistress. This was a large conservatory on the left of the front door. Judging from old engravings, it must have shown the same indecision in style as the rest of the house, its low-pitched roof decorated with urns, making it more like a Georgian orangery than the soaring glass cathedrals that were built a little later in the century.

In 1846 there was yet more building, this time for Walter's convenience. Stretching to the right of the façade and still in the same Tudor-cum-Regency style, he built a library wing with a new master bedroom and dressing-room above. Perhaps because his heart and imagination – and convenience – were very much in the project, the library turned out to be the most beautiful room in the house. One large bay window looks straight out over the sea to Wales; the other faces east along the wooded cliffs to Porlock Bay and Hurlestone Point. The fireplace is baronial dark oak, locally carved and incorporating older figures, but the pleasant character of the room comes from the fact that the mahogany book-shelves and the oak doors curve gently so that there are no corners and one is comfortably wrapped round in books.

The library was a necessity rather than an indulgence because Walter was an avid book collector. He never, unfortunately, brought Gibbon's library back to England, and it was sold when the Château des Clées was given up but, even so, judging by dates on fly leaves, he had a large collection before 1846. In later accounts, £1000 is put down as being spent on the library, the same sum as on the wine-cellar, and there was very little room for the books of succeeding generations at his death. He was never tempted to buy up another whole library; the books were collected individually and, as he tended to put the place and date of his purchase on the fly leaves, one can almost follow him through the bookshops of Europe.

A person's books are always supposed to be a good indication of character as well as interests. It is difficult to apply this to Walter and the only safe conclusion one can come to is that he seemed to be interested in anything in print and, while he had obvious antiquarian interests, he also liked the latest! As befitted an educated gentleman of the period, there is a sizeable classical section of English and French editions, mostly from the late eighteenth and early nineteenth centuries, starting with the *Gradus ad Parnassum* and *An Introduction to the Latin Tongue for the use of Youth* dated 'Eton College 1809' but long after he could safely have considered his formal education at an end he was still collecting editions of the classics.

One remembers that he was in Holy Orders and looks for clues to his tastes and beliefs in the theological section. By all accounts, he was Broad Church rather than anything else but, if the choice had been forced on him, he would have been Low rather than High. However, one could never guess this from his books. There are some beautiful old editions of the early fathers: a St Clement of Alexandria in Greek and Latin, published in 1715, a St Cyril of 1620, a St Bernard of 1690 and a St Cyprian of 1700. There is also a Eusebius of 1709 and a beautiful vellum-bound Bede of 1722 in Latin and Anglo-Saxon. Of course, one could well dismiss these as showing antiquarian rather than theological interests but there are still some odd neighbours on the shelves. Paley's *Evidences* and Dupin's *History of the Church* were accepted reading but one feels one might be getting down to particular interests when one finds 39 volumes of the Parker Society publications. The Parker Society was instituted in 1840 for the publication of works of the Fathers and Early Writers of the Reformed English Church and Walter's name is on the list of subscribers – but the pages are uncut! Again, one feels one might be getting somewhere with *Peranzabulo* which Trelawny Collins produced in 1837 to prove that the Celtic, not the Roman, was the original true Church, and this is followed by *Roman Forgeries – Impostures of the Church of Rome* published in 1673, and the *Tears, Sighs, Complaints and Prayers of the Church of England* published in 1659 but, a little further along the shelf, is a Roman Breviary of 1750 bought in Rome in 1844. He had Sir Isaac Newton's *Observations on Daniel and Revelations*, but he also had the Reverend Edward Irving's *Discourses on the Prophecies of Daniel and Revelations* and his *Orations on Judgement to Come* although he was certainly no Irvingite. *The Enthusiasms of the Methodists and Papists Compared* are also on the same shelf and could be taken to suggest that he disliked excess. It is certain, however, from evidence other than his library that he was a good, practising Christian and, from his journal, one discovers that he always observed Sunday on his travels, going to Church if possible, and reading the morning and evening services if not. He always commented, if he had been to Church, on how well the lessons and prayers were read but this, of course, could be put down to professional interest. It is probably safe to conclude that he was middle-of-the-road Church of England himself, but was either scholar enough to want to know what he disagreed with or was simply interested in other people and what inspired them.

He certainly did not disapprove of novels; the shelves are full of them. As one might expect, there seems to be everything that Scott wrote, often duplicated, and there is also a good deal of what came to be known as Scottiana, but then Scott was a distinguished compatriot as well as the most popular novelist of his time. There are nearly all the novels that Jane Austen's heroines read, starting with three nice editions of the *Mysteries of Udolpho* and *The Italian* in both English and French: the French copy was bought in 1815 when Walter was staying in the 'Bologna Hotel de San Marco'. There are, predictably, M.G. Lewis' *The Monk* and *Tales of Terror*, but there is also *A Sicilian Romance* and the *Romance of the Forest – Interspersed with pieces of Poetry, The Old English Baron* and *Le Naufrage – traduit de l'Anglais de Miss F.H. Burney*. Were the French translations bought as relatively painless ways of improving one's French? Maria Edgeworth is well represented and all of Jane Austen used to be there in first editions. New novels seem to have been collected as they came out. A little further along the shelves there seems to be nearly everything that John Galt and Fenimore Cooper wrote, as well as a collection of almost forgotten writers like C.R. Maturin and John Moore. There is, however, an equally good collection of the earlier writers: Dr Johnson, Smollett, Fielding, Goldsmith and John Gay are all there. Later on, Dickens was added as his novels came out in monthly parts. In fact, it is a most complete library for the student of English literature.

There seem to be countless biographies and collections of letters of long forgotten people, and one is tempted to think that some at least were dutifully bought, but there are two collections of books which do show a more specialised interest and neither of them seems quite what one might expect. The first shows a deep interest in seventeenth-century English history.

There are various books on the life and times, and courts, of the Stuart kings, books on Cromwell and his Parliaments, a life of General Monck, Memoirs of Judge Jeffreys, Laud's memorials, and three seventeenth-century books on Archbishop Laud: Heylin's *Life*, Prynne's *Breviate of the Life of Laud* and the *History of the Commitment and Trial*. The interest seems to have been historical rather than literary for, except for Milton, the Metaphysicals are not represented at all, either in poetry or prose. Walter's other particular interest appeared to be in the French

Revolution and, on a high and generally rather dusty shelf, is his collection of French paperbacks with titles such as *L'Histoire de la Terreur, Mémoires de Lucien Bonaparte, Histoire des Insurrections de Lyons, Mémoires de Marie Capelle veuve Lafarge, L'Ancien Regime et la Revolution, Louis XVI, Marie Antoinette et Mme Elizabeth*. The revolution must have dominated his youth but it is interesting that, in later life, he set out to find out about it in such detail. In passing, it is interesting to note that an 1822 edition of Boccaccio's *Decameron* has survived, perhaps because it, too, is on a very high shelf.

As with the furnishing of the house, it is difficult to sum up the library tidily: there is such variety and, with the exception of the Parker Society volumes, it is obviously well used. It seems safe to conclude, in the light of what one learns about his character, that Walter's own basic ideas, particularly those of religion and philosophy, were formed on the Bible and the Classics without too much thought and taken for granted, but that he was endlessly interested in what inspired and informed other people. His 'new' ideas were concerned with the art of living, not with questioning any basic beliefs.

FRILLS AND FURBELOWS

Simultaneously, other essential buildings were going up. After the first mile of drive, one rounds a sharp corner through the main gate and comes upon the lodge, first built in the 1830s and altered in the 1850s. The gate pillars are simple, topped by large boars' heads, crisply carved in Portland stone, and they are rather elegant. The lodge, however, shows strong Robinson influence and is, undeniably, an ornamental cottage with heavily latticed windows, ornamental barge-boards and fish scale tiles. Looking at it from across the combe, one half expects gnomes to emerge.

At the bottom of the combe, at a suitable distance from the house, and invisible from it, is the original home farm, a substantial building with pretty leaded windows and two wings, one of stables and hay loft, the other of cow stalls and storage space, forming a snug courtyard. When another building of shippon and more stables was built, and then another for kennels and pigsties, followed by a wash and brew house, hen-house, laundry and coach-house, all in the same style, this began to look like a separate, busy hamlet. When the fruit trees began to grow up by the pond, this patch must have looked efficiently tamed but, as a reminder that nature here was paramount, successive flooding of the pretty stream washed out the pond and made one range of buildings so dangerous that they had to be demolished.

The home farm took care of a lot of the household's needs but, further along the cliff and about as far away as the home farm in another direction, a kitchen garden was created to provide fruit, vegetables and cut flowers. High walls were built to enclose almost an acre of gently sloping ground. Glasshouses were put up all along the south wall and, at one end of this wall on its outer, northern side, was built the gardener's cottage. Like the lodge, it is undeniably ornamental and, although it is also what is known on Exmoor as 'back-sunned', it has a beautiful view through its leaded bay window in the parlour. A path winds past it along the cliff, stopping abruptly at the best point for watching the sun sink into the waters of the Bristol Channel or, as Walter and his contemporaries would have thought of it, the Severn Sea. It is most likely that the gardener availed himself of this amenity less than most people because, at dusk, he was probably stoking the furnaces that heated the glasshouses where the grapes, peaches, nectarines and pineapples grew. None the less, the kitchen garden, though now bereft of its glasshouses, box hedges and espalier trees, has still a striking beauty and serenity.

As far from the house in the opposite direction, an ice-house was made according to the instructions in Loudon's *Manual on Gardening*. It was constructed in the steep bank of another little stream running down another narrow combe. It consisted of a tunnel winding into the bank to a deep, cemented pit which held the ice. It was sealed by two tightly fitting doors to keep out any warm air, and it ensured a supply of ice throughout the year to make ice puddings and to keep the fish fresh. Sometimes the fish came by coach from Exeter, so it may have been in need of ice as soon as it arrived but, in the season, Glenthorne had its own fish from a weir constructed on the shore below the ice-house combe. This weir was made by building a stout stone wall to enclose a square 'field' just below high water mark. When the tide retreated, it left the fish high and dry to be picked up for consumption. Walter must have been proud of his weir for its completion was celebrated by tea for all at the Blue Ball to the accompaniment of a German band. It must certainly have been well constructed for its remains are still there after more than a century's neglect by all but the battering tides.

The weir and ice-house were later conveniences but, very early in the whole enterprise, a jetty was made on the same stretch of rocky beach as the weir. It must have made the dispossessed smugglers envious. Porlock Hill was an almost insurmountable barrier to the transport of heavy goods by road so they came round by sea. Some building materials came by road as far as Porlock Bay and were then shipped but, twice a year until 1929, the coal came straight across the Channel from Wales. Even so, it was a three-day operation. On the first day the lugger stood off while the men cleared the beach of the larger and more awkward stones and, on the second and third days, the cargo was unloaded, then stored in the coal-house built, in matching style, against the cliff at the back of the landing stage. From there, it was taken by horse and cart, as it was needed, to the house and cottages. On one side of the coal-house, Walter built a boat-house, its upper storey snugly equipped with a little fireplace. On the other side was a limekiln for the lime used for dressing the acid soil of the fields. The limestone was also brought in by boat and burned there before the result was carted 1000 feet up to the farms. All these conveniences were made after the latest models, but they all needed a great deal of patient man and horse power!

There were a few more frivolous buildings, too, although none of them were on the grand scale of eighteenth-century temples, belvederes and hermitages. There was a functional coach-house beside the stables but, near the bottom of the drive, another one was built with a wide flat-arched doorway flanked by two ridiculous little towers with roofs like witches' hats. One had a false door and the other a door that opens on nothing but the hillside.

On an elbow bend of the path leading from the garden to the beach, a bath-house was built. Its main room was octagonal with a little fireplace and a leaded window which looked over the sea. It was furnished with a rustic table, chair and stool, a cast from the Capitol, and a hip bath. Here, invigorating sea-water baths were taken in warmth and comfort, the essential sea-water being hauled up the steep path in buckets by perspiring servants. In a little, lower room was, most improbably, a water closet and the whole charming little building was capped by a groined roof and tall chimney. It was tucked into the hillside and surrounded by trees but one day one of the trees fell on top of it and now its existence is remembered only by a rubbish-filled hole in the ground. Once there was a tea house just above the bath-house and, higher up the hill where the view was even more spectacular, a summer house, but these were rustic, wooden buildings and now only flattened patches of earth and a few slates remain.

There is, however, one folly which still appears to be very sturdy. On one of the lower elbows of the drive stands a noble archway with a small stone lion comfortably couched above it. It is flanked by solid, round-capped towers, roughly Norman in feeling and on top of each one stands an heraldic stone bird a little larger than the lion which appears to have goose somewhere in its ancestry. In spite of its weighty construction there is something light-hearted about this gateway – a feeling one gets frequently about the whole estate. The only really awkward circumstance about 'The Towers' is that they look as though they guard the pathway to somewhere important, possibly the house itself. People have understandably set off that way, only to find themselves on a precipitous path leading, apparently endlessly, along a spectacular, but utterly lonely stretch of cliff. Valerian and fern have rooted themselves in the landward tower, destructive no doubt, but adding to the picturesque nature of the place and for a long time the seaward tower was inhabited by an old sheep thought by some frivolous persons to be the spirit of Wordsworth.

One might have thought that this, even though it was spread over years, would have been enough building for one man but Walter was energetic and he liked building. When he started building Glenthorne he sold his property in Lynmouth but he could not resist buying some land that was on offer further up the valley behind the town. His only reason was that in a picturesquely beautiful landscape this area was still noticeably exciting. The river valley behind Lynmouth burrows narrowly into the surrounding high hills. The road that goes up it to the high windswept and marshy common is still narrow and winding and has been blasted in places through solid red rock but, in 1830, when Walter was building there, there was only a narrow path, little better than a sheep track at times. In places, the valley bottom is narrow enough to be almost a gorge but here and there it opens out a little. It widens out at one point where two fast streams, the East Lyn River and Hoaroak Water, cascade over the rocks to meet and flow down to the sea. Here Walter built Watersmeet Cottage as a fishing lodge. It is quite a small cottage and would have won Robinson's wholehearted approval.

It is composed of a central octagon with narrow rectangular wings on either side with the kitchen quarters tucked away behind. The gables have ornamental barge-boards, the windows are Gothic and there is a rustic porch, originally thatched and supported by 'rude oak posts', running along the river frontage. Contemporary prints make the whole area look almost frightening, but Walter and Katherine seemed to go over quite regularly to ruralise in even greater solitude than they enjoyed at Glenthorne and, in May of 1832, Katherine tells Bessey that they have just held a gala there. She does not enlarge on this so we do not know what form it took, but they must have had a number of equally intrepid friends and neighbours. Every year they spent the whole of April there while Glenthorne was spring-cleaned. It was, I suppose, the usual spring-cleaning time anyway, but it is a marvellous time of year to be at Watersmeet when the rivers are still full, the trees fresh green and the sun high enough to shine into the combe.

As there were no heirlooms to be accommodated and no style to be kept up, Walter was able to indulge himself completely in the furnishing of Watersmeet as well as the building and be, according to his ideas, thoroughly cottagey. Practically everything was made of oak and, wherever possible, carved. In the best octagon bedroom there was, according to the inventory: a carved oak bedstead, a carved oak dressing-table, a long swing-glass in a carved oak stand, a carved oak wardrobe, a carved oak washing-stand, three oak chairs, and two old pictures. Later, most of these things were removed to one of the biggest Glenthorne bedrooms and, even with more space and light around them, the result was nightmarish. In fact, the bedstead, a heavy four-poster, achieved a little fame by featuring in a painting by Sir Alfred Munnings. Beside the bed was a translucent white figure and its title was 'The Nightmare'. The bed was made entirely of carved oak and had been put together from assorted bits of old carving by a cabinet maker working in Exeter Cathedral Yard. Its transport, even if it was finally assembled 'on site', must have been quite an effort. Since the beginning of this century it had been abandoned by all but the mice who nested securely at the bottom of its hollow Gothic posts; then some years ago, it was discovered that all but the hardest wood was infested by furniture beetle, death-watch beetle and rot, so it had to be dismantled.

Even if the original furnishing of the cottage was too exuberantly Tudoresque for our present taste, the cottage itself is undeniably an aesthetic success. Whether one likes the sentimental and picturesque or not, one must agree that the building fits beautifully into its surroundings and, by its smallness of scale and slightly cosy air, adds, by contrast, to the wildness of the natural scene. It provides all the sentimental associations, too, of a lodge in the wilderness offering a safe though humble haven for the traveller – preferably benighted! All lovers of the picturesque are still delighted by it.

For some time now, Watersmeet has belonged to the National Trust, so its preservation in the way that its creator intended is as certain as anything can be. Anyone who can, or will, manage the steep walk to the cottage may now enjoy tea on the small lawn by the river as Walter and Katherine did, although on a fine afternoon in the season it may seem like one of their gala days and there is some irony in the sight of numbers of people standing in front of the door to read the quotation from Wordsworth carved on a stone plaque over it:

The spot was made by Nature for herself;
The travellers know it not, and 'twill remain
Unknown to them; but it is beautiful;
And if a man should plant his cottage near,
Should sleep beneath the shelter of its trees,
And blend its waters with his daily meal,
He would so love it, that in his death hour
Its image would survive among his thoughts.

Even now, on the busiest day, one gets the feeling that nature is in command, particularly if one has memories of the Lynmouth flood.

Whatever one might feel about the style of architecture favoured in all these new buildings, one has to concede that a serious and well-considered effort has been made to fit them into the landscape, and that a certain sort of modesty was shown in the way that none of them set out to dominate their environment. There is modesty, too, in the scale of building: even the big house is small as big houses of the period went, and it is built with human requirements in mind, not as an assertion of self-importance. Even though there was a general movement away from the grandeur of neo-classical architecture back to what was considered the more modest indigenous style, there was still plenty of scope if one had a taste for grandeur: one merely 'went medieval' and built a vast castle in which to live. Walter favoured the Tudor mode because it seemed to him that its intention was domestic and its disposition was to serve rather than to dominate. The Tudor idea, however, did not extend outside the house. Certain conveniences like farmyards and kitchen gardens were necessary to support life but, otherwise, one interfered with nature as little as possible. Formal gardens had been abandoned when Georgian architecture became the fashion, but now even the more natural contrivances of Kent and Capability Brown were condemned as altogether too tame. Walter built a terrace with Bath stone balustrades round the house for a safe, level walk was considered a necessity but apart from that, as little as possible was done. The land below and round the terrace sloped naturally to the cliff edge and this was kept scythed, but only the odd tree was planted and the occasional rustic bench placed in a convenient position for resting the legs and refreshing the eyes. The stream which supplied the house water runs close through a steep-sided channel until it falls to the beach, and a walk was cut along it but nothing else done except discreet trimming. Now there is a formal rose garden between the terrace and the cliff top, a croquet lawn at one side, edged by a flower border and little flower beds by the house walls. The paths by the stream have been extended too and a great deal of planting done to make a water garden, but all these were later Victorian and Edwardian additions. Originally, only ivy grew up the house walls drawing the deer to feed on it at dusk. Flowers for the house were grown within the wall of the kitchen garden and the short grass near the house merged imperceptibly with the meadows and the trees.

Further from the house the treatment was the same. A chain of ponds was made down the combe, partly to regulate the water flow for safety's sake, partly for decoration and, in the case of the one near the farm, for convenience. But they were all left entirely 'unimproved' and even the dams are not easily recognised as such. Behind the lodge, busts were placed as guardians of the spring for Walter could never lose his classical upbringing and in a little clearing below, more classical statuary rose above the ferns. Much labour was employed to make miles of pathways through the combes and along the cliffs. Many of them are most beautifully faced with stones set in the banks in the local manner, even in places where it must have been dangerous to push a wheelbarrow. Here and there, where it was judged that a seat would be pleasant, flat stones or slates were let into the bank, but there are only two points where there has been any building more ambitious. In one place, a semi-circular wall has been built round a seat and, on Desolation Point, there is a little Gothic look-out. It is a fine place for a look-out post, but one feels that Walter was probably inspired by the very name and felt that it ought to be given importance.

A good deal of tree planting went on, not in the clumps and belts that Capability Brown recommended (in any case there were no suitable vistas for this treatment) but in the way that Uvedale Price advocated and that we still approve – that of managing and regenerating existing woodlands and species of trees and discreetly adding to them. Early prints show some quite bare cliffs and hillsides: now the place is lost in trees, mostly oaks, and some of them are, by now, old and twisted enough for the most romantic mind. In one place, however, Walter departed from the natural and planted himself a pinetum. Evergreen trees brought from the East and from the New World were still very new, and Veitch of Exeter was one of the earliest collectors. The Aclands commissioned him to plant the fine collection at Killerton and it was from him that the Glenthorne seeds and saplings came and were planted in the well protected combe above the ice-house, merging up its sides with the natural trees. It is not a very big collection: there is a far bigger and finer one not too far away at Bicton, as well as at Killerton. Neglect in the war years, storm and age have all had their effect, but there are still some fine old specimens which have reached a great height. The pride of the collection, however, was planted on the cliff edge, right in front of the house. It is a stone-pine and, throughout the last century, its progress seems to have been followed with care and regularly measured, for old notebooks have turned up from time to time recording its 'vital statistics' at different dates. There is still a stone-pine in the same position but, though it is old enough to need its limbs propping up, it must be a successor to the original one. One wonders if Walter was conscious of betraying his ideal of nothing but the natural in planting these very new trees and, indeed, if his interest in the newest often got in the way of his cultivation of the old and natural, but then I suppose the old and natural were in themselves part of the newest ideas.

While many of the new rich of the period were creating seats for themselves whose newness was their most obvious and prided recommendation, Walter's antiquarian interests seem to have moved him to the creation of a legend. Having built a house that was intended to deceive the eye into assuming that it had been there for ages, it seems as if he set about reinforcing the idea with names. He carefully collected and recorded the names that existed such as Tapster Ridge, Brandy Path, Horritor and Horror Slade; this last, a path along the cliff where three members of one family disappeared, at different times, over the edge. Then he added a few more of his own. The name of the house itself sets the tone. It is built at the bottom of Coscombe and, in an earlier generation, it would probably have become Coscombe House or possibly just Countisbury Manor, but he obviously required something with more atmosphere. There is an abundance of thorn trees in the combe and he was, after all, a Scot so it became

Glenthorne. One hill to the east of the house, because of its shape, became Sugarloaf and a nearby plantation became Cocked Hat Wood. Where one of the springs emerges, Walter placed a marble trough from Scio and built a sort of stone beehive over it, topped it with a rude stone cross and called it Sisters' Well after his four little nieces. For some forgotten reason, the path leading up to it is called Valentine's and on one corner of the drive there is Celia's Seat, although we no longer know who Celia was or why she sat there. This deliberate attempt to create a legendary atmosphere has borne some fruit. Stories have since grown up about smuggling and hunting here and even the supernatural. From somewhere the legend sprang up that Joseph of Arimathea had landed in Glenthorne Cove when trading up the coast and, striking the ground with his staff, he had brought forth a spring at the Sisters' Fountain which never runs dry. Who knows, the story went on, perhaps Christ was also in the boat on his way to bring the Glastonbury Thorn into being? Strangely, no one except Munnings has ever even tried to suggest a ghost and it seems impossible to imagine anything in the least eerie, even when alone on a wild night in this isolated building. Whether one puts this down to the basic sweetness and sanity of its creator or the basic solidity of his descendants, is a matter for conjecture.

Walter must have discovered quite soon that elegant simplicity was expensive. Even though he employed no famous name in architecture or landscape design and had no agent to collect his books, marbles and pictures, the basic house had cost £12,000 by 1831 and the later building and furnishing added another £8000. Watersmeet cost £1000 to build, apart from the cost of the land (another £1000) and of the rustic furnishing. It was a big sum of money for what was considered quite a modest house. But he was a very rich man, after all, and had lost no energy and gained no care in acquiring his fortune. He had merely to enjoy it, which he did, initially, with an exuberance which can still be felt. The place has posed apparently insoluble problems to all his successors but those who merely visit it are almost invariably struck with the mixture of pleasantness and excitement which it exudes.

So this solid paradox grew; a well-built, large, modern house, that still managed to look modest – and old – in the middle of wild solitude, fitted with all modern conveniences and up-to-date gadgets and surrounded with cheerful bits of nonsense, most of which had been constructed with considerable expense and labour. It was assumed that it would run with the same civilised smoothness as anything in the Home Counties and it provided a delightful haven for those who enjoyed the feeling of being solitaries in trackless waste without denying themselves any reasonable creature comforts. It had solidity and has proved its durability but spiritually it was a confection, and it was also an instant legend.

GOOD COMPANY

Walter enjoyed sharing his solitude. In 1832 he was writing with his usual enthusiasm to entice Nash Hilliard down: 'It is only', he says, 'two days' journey, and it would give us great pleasure to show you how happily we live, remote from cities, and when you have *once* seen Glenthorne you will cease to wonder at our disinclination to leave it.' One summer, not long afterwards, Katherine was writing to Bessey Hilliard to say that were fully 'booked' right through until October!

It appears that friends and relations were only too ready to be enticed to Glenthorne and a charming picture of life in the wilds of Exmoor is given in a book of reminiscences printed for private circulation in 1897. The book is *Reminiscences and Reflections of an Old West Country Clergyman.* Its writer, W.S. Thornton, was sent when he was seventeen to be prepared for Cambridge by Mr Hoare, the curate of Selworthy, and spent two happy years there getting to know the country and its inhabitants, as well as Latin and Greek. During that time, he became so attached to the place that he returned later to be the unpaid curate to the vicar of Lynton, and to take sole charge of Countisbury for twenty pounds a year.

His account of Glenthorne is, no doubt, tinged by the afterglow of happy recollection, but his enjoyment must have been real enough. His first introduction to the West Country, he says, had been when he first visited Glenthorne in 1837, 'and there, as a nursery child, had made the acquaintance of the highly gifted, kindly and eccentric owner, who was destined in after years to be my squire and lifelong and valued friend.' It was in 1847, however, that he came to Selworthy and really got to know the place and its owner. 'I was continually at Glenthorne', he writes. 'At all hours of the day and night my poor pony was traversing either the lower path through Ashley Lodge and Culbone Wood, or the lane through the farms above, or the high road by Hurlestone Rocks. Mr Halliday was kindness itself and an old friend of the Thornton family ... He was a very remarkable man, of shy, retiring habits, very plain, with a marvellous play of countenance, full of wit and anecdote, a great traveller and very hospitable. Mrs Halliday was always kind, and I had the run of the house.'

'Glenthorne, however, possessed another attraction. It was continually being visited by people of distinction. Old naval officers, who had fought with Nelson and Dundonald, would there hold me enthralled with tales of the great war in which they themselves had played a distinguished part. Conspicuous among these was one who, when he died, was Admiral of the Fleet, Sir Fairfax Moresby, G.C.B. He had, as he said, "commanded everything afloat from a cockleshell to a Fleet of Line of Battle-Ships." He had cruised with Cochrane in the *Speedy*, and had been with Nelson at Trafalgar.'

'He honoured the Rugby boy (Thornton himself) with a friendship which, for thirty years, never flagged or failed, until I stood by his open grave in Littleham Churchyard and reverently helped to commit to earth the ashes of the veteran of ninety-one who had served his King and his country for seventy-eight long years.'

'To Glenthorne also came the Knights from Simonsbath – Frederic Charles, and Lewis – and there I made their acquaintance. Sir Frederic still survives, and it is necessary to be careful, but I will venture to say that for wild and reckless daring I have never known the equals of that triumvirate. Age may, by that time, have cooled them a little, but if they were cool when I first knew them what must they have been at an earlier date, ere the eldest had married and entered Parliament; the second been much crippled by a fall in the Roman Campagna; and the third tossed nine times by a buffalo cow in the depths of remotest Abyssinia!'

'The Hallidays had no children of their own, but their house used often to be well filled with young people, more especially in the Summer, when Lady Cosway (born Halliday) was wont to bring down her four daughters from Cowes, and the two Miss Moresbys would be there. The supply of rough ponies was apparently inexhaustible, and the young pupils from Selworthy, ten miles away, frequently assisted the ladies to explore the whole wild Exmoor Forest, and other places besides. I, at least, was often in the company of the girls, with whom, so far as the Cosways were concerned, I was already intimate, as they had been in Surrey the playmates of my infancy.'

'And must I here pause to describe Glenthorne itself, this bright resort of my opening life?'

52

'No!   It is now well known to the ever-increasing stream of strangers who throng our West Country lanes from June to October, and I will content myself with narrating that it is a good country house, built on a little meadow some eighty feet above the shore of the Bristol Channel, and three miles by road from the lofty crest of a hill which extends unbroken from Countisbury to above Porlock. It is seven miles from Lynmouth.'

'The house, facing to the East, is surrounded by good gardens, and from it ramify and spread upwards many paths and trackways which conduct the traveller to varied scenes of marvellous beauty. Admiral Moresby used often to assert that nowhere in the world, save only on the coasts of Catalonia, can you find such long stretches of luxuriant wood clothing the steep hillsides right down to the water's edge.'

Reading this enthusiastic account, one does rather wonder why a shy, retiring, scholarly man should create the perfect home for a recluse, then fill it with healthy extroverts and proceed to be the life and soul of the party.

Presumably his romantic habits were comparative rather than absolute and he was only quiet and scholarly compared with the rest of his family. The elderly sailors who so often visited him were his father's friends whom he must have known all his life and, after all, he and his nieces and the intrepid Miss Moresbys were all children of similar naval gentlemen. It is probably true to say that he was not so much a shy man as a private one. He did not want permanent solitude, but had no interest in the world of Parliament, place-seeking and mass entertainment for influence or show. His house was isolated and had no suite of 'public' rooms for receptions or balls but it was big enough to accommodate plenty of friends and there was enough floor space for an impromptu dance! The surrounding natural beauty was felt to be a delight quite as much as a means of moral uplift. It was, in fact, the good life as prescribed by Maria Edgeworth and Jane Austen.

As a youth of seventeen, escaping from his books, Thornton would naturally be drawn to the vigorous and lively visitors but many who came were distinguished for quieter pursuits. From time to time one comes across books in the library signed by the authors in memory of happy days at Glenthorne. Most of the names have long since been forgotten but, among them, Southey is still remembered. Among the artists – and would-be artists –

who came, the most distinguished were the Severns, father and son, and Walter Severn left portraits of Walter, Katherine, their niece Helen, and of the house, which still hang in their places. Walter himself wrote occasional, light verse, congratulations on birthdays or lines accompanying little presents, which are surprisingly eighteenth century in flavour. They have a kindly charm but are otherwise totally undistinguished.

In general, Walter must have been well pleased with the life he had created for himself. Even so, in the midst of his well-chosen company, he felt the occasional desire for an escape to solitude and his new house could supply even this need. The study is a long room at the top of the front stairs with an oriel window over the front door. From here he had early warning of arriving visitors and, if he decided against company, he went quickly up an elegant little flight of stairs in one corner and disappeared into the attic above. The attic is completely cut off from the rest of the top floor and can be reached in no other way. It was obviously intended as a stack room and muniment store and has bookshelves fitted all round it and a slit window above the oriel on the floor below. No doubt the door over the top of the stairs was originally put there to stop draughts, but it made it a more secure retreat and it has always been known as the bolt hole. Here Walter could sit and read until he felt more sociable or could see from the little window that the coast was clear. It was an admirable convenience.

THE PRACTICAL SIDE OF ROMANTICISM

If this had been the full extent of Walter's enterprise, he could have settled down in early middle age to years of kindly hedonism but so far he had used only his personal legacy plus a small borrowing from his main entailed inheritance. There was still the brewery concern, the Scottish estate of Whinnyrig, the Jamaican estate of Castle Wemyss and the main sum of money, about £70,000, to be considered. He had no desire to make more money but he could not escape looking after what he already had and, even if he did his best to ignore some of his responsibilities, there was his busy, businesslike co-executor and brother-in-law, Sir William Cosway, to keep him up to the mark.

For some time before his death, Simon had been pulling out of the brewery business in Ipswich, but progress was slow. The public houses could be sold only as buyers offered and the claims of the dependants of the deceased partner had to be settled. It even took some time to retrieve the books from the bankrupt partner who had gone to France in a great hurry. However, it was not too long a journey for William to go to Ipswich to try to find out how matters stood and then it was largely a question of time and apparently interminable correspondence with the lawyers who were managing the whole affair.

The Scottish estate provided no particular complications in itself. It had been in the hands of an agent for a long time, but Walter had decided to hand over the income to Katherine for her life and, as Scottish law differed in some aspects from English, this had to be a separate transaction. Other anxieties were nearly all caused, or at least exaggerated, by distance and lack of familiarity. Correspondence about rents, or lack of them, was slow and it was difficult to assess the need for repairs and alterations without an uncomfortably great dependence on the agent. There were always crises when someone's outhouse was collapsing, or the tides were breaking down the sea walls, or a tenant was begging for more time to pay. Once again time generally settled these problems. The indefatigable Sir William went up to Dumfriesshire and enquired into affairs very thoroughly and, thereafter, Walter and Katherine would go up occasionally and at leisure, making a holiday of the excursion and visiting their relations.

The Jamaican estate was much more of a liability and its problems were apparently insoluble, nor could any useful purpose be served by a long sea voyage out there to inspect it. Ever since England had lost the sugar monopoly it had been difficult to make a satisfactory profit and Simon, with all his attention to business, had felt the acquisition of Castle Wemyss an infliction, but he did still receive some income from it, although this declined steadily.

In 1832, however, when the anti-slavery Bill was finally passed, the whole Jamaican economy collapsed. Vast numbers of newly freed slaves disappeared into the unsettled and unexplored jungle in the middle of the island where they lived as best they could. They were little worse off for food than they had been on the estates and at least, they did virtually no work for it. They had never had much in the way of possessions so they did not miss those. From time to time they made forays to the estates to steal what they could, burn down the mills and refineries and occasionally murder anyone they had a particular spite against, that is if they had not thoughtfully done these jobs before they went. They were, after all, working off years of bitter resentment. Those who chose to stay behind demanded exorbitant wages for unreliable work. Walter was as much in favour of freedom for the slaves as anyone, but that did nothing to solve his immediate problems. From time to time, Sir William wrote to Walter saying that something must be done about the West Indian estate and, at one point, Walter must have replied suggesting that, if they shut their eyes, it might go away, for Sir William wrote back saying that, if nothing was done 'certain persons' might come upon the executors for dilapidations.

Various young men, caught out in Jamaica at the time of abolition and with no other prospects, took on the hopeless job of trying to manage the estate and it was permanently up for sale. At Simon's death, its estimated value had already dropped from £23,000 to £14,000. When it was finally sold, in 1864, it fetched £550! Time, and the lawyers, dealt with these problems, but there was still the investment of the Trust Fund to be considered. If Walter had wanted a quiet life more than anything else, he would have done well to have left the money in Government Securities and lived off the income. Although they seemed to agree on remarkably few points, both he and Sir William were convinced that the fortune should be invested in land. For a long time after this, land was considered the only safe investment and a man was not really a true gentleman unless he was a landed one. William and Walter may have agreed on this point but it became immediately apparent that they could not possibly agree on where this land was to be found. They started to argue about it almost immediately and went on for years, with Walter's solicitor, poor Nash Hilliard, caught in the cross-fire.

In November 1830 Sir William Cosway wrote to Nash Hilliard: 'I am favoured with your letter relative to the probable sale of an Estate in Gloucestershire ... I have communicated with Mr Halliday on the propriety of investing the Trust Fund in hand at the present moment – but he wishes the investment to be made in Somersetshire or Devonshire – so as to be within reasonable distance of Lynton. As he has a right to have his wishes consulted, I have only to regret that his selection may throw difficulties in the way of a suitable and speedy purchase.'

In 1832, Katherine Halliday in a business letter to Hilliard, says: 'Thanks for letting me know of the Estate for sale in Dorset.' Early in 1833 Walter wrote to him about the possibility of buying one of the Acland estates near Bridgwater 'or', he adds, 'one in Herefordshire, a favourite County of mine.' The mention of the Bridgwater estate was reasonably serious but one suspects that of Herefordshire was merely self-assertion. Sir William might have been exasperated, but he was not to be diverted. In April 1833 he wrote to Hilliard: 'There is an estate in E. Kent of about £40,000 I apprehend, of the best land in the County, called Grove, near Wingham. The owner, Mr Brockman, is lately dead, and it will be disposed of to be divided among the younger children.' The next month Walter wrote to Hilliard disposing, as he thought, of that one: 'I have received a letter from Sir William Cosway mentioning the Estate in Kent, which County is too far removed from my property here to be thought of for an instant ...' and Katherine wrote to Mrs Hilliard: 'Walter wishes Mr Hilliard to be on the look-out for a *good*, that is a profitable Estate, – he is partial to Herefordshire – in which case he requests Mr Hilliard to be on the look-out for land in that neighbourhood – Mr Law, solicitor in

New Square, Lincolns Inn, will give him all particulars of an Estate now for sale in that County.'

Two months later, Sir William is still doing his best to recommend the estate in Kent, and writes a long, irritated letter to poor Mr Hilliard about it: 'I apprehend the residue of the late Mr Halliday's Estate should be invested in land in the most advantageous way, without having to do with the picturesque – but giving that fair preference to the tenant for life as to locality which common sense and reason could point out.' He then states his reasons for preferring Kent and goes on to say: 'These are my principal reasons for recommending you to apply to Messrs Fosters about the Grove Estate – it is the same Estate mentioned before – but I do my duty as a trustee in proposing an investment whenever I think there is a good one. The distance from London is also an advantage for who is to manage an Estate in Herefordshire, or any of the distant Counties – neither Mr Halliday nor myself are near it – and to buy an Estate merely because it may be pretty to look at once in ten years – is no reason to be offered to others. The Grove Estate I know to be some of the best land in the County.'

A month after receiving this letter from William, Nash Hilliard wrote diplomatically to Walter about Walter's suggestion of the Acland estate in Somerset or one in Herefordshire: 'Between ourselves, I fully expect that Sir William will prove an unwilling purchaser in either of those Counties – but this we must not regard when an eligible opportunity offers, and there seem inducements to give the preference to the Estate of Sir Thos. Acland. In his last letter upon urging the purchase of the Grove Estate in Kent, Sir William expressed many sentiments which induced me to form this opinion.'

It is difficult to see how the situation was ever to be resolved. Basically Walter was determined to have something reasonably near to his beloved Glenthorne although he was also enjoying the feeling that he could buy land anywhere in the British Isles. Among his papers there are even particulars of an estate in Southwest Wales which sounds a very poor investment, but he may have shown an interest in this merely to annoy Sir William. Sir William, in any case, had reached the point where he despised and distrusted any suggestion of Walter's. Even when Walter was inclined to buy a town house in St James' which must have seemed a faultless investment, William wrote to Hilliard: 'I have

58

seen the exterior of the house in St James' Place which *I* do not like. Mr Halliday may, and as I wrote to you before, it being a matter of taste he must decide for himself.' This had been Walter's view of the whole matter all along! Sir William was dutifully fighting the cause of common sense, although there was a dash of self-interest in the background. It was obviously sensible to buy good land and equally sensible to buy soon for England was recovering from the slump following the war and it was still possible to buy relatively cheaply. Nevertheless, as far as his preference for Kent was concerned, he was, no doubt, expecting to do much of the managing himself in the hope that it might eventually be for his son.

This clash of ideals did nothing to improve their relations in other ways. Walter disapproved strongly of his brother-in-law's powers of legalistic argument and, as early as 1831, was referring to him as 'a great Jesuit' and writing to Nash Hilliard: ' ... I have no doubt that if I died Sir William would claim the Banking House profits for his wife as heir-at-law as he would have done with the Scotch Property.' By June 1834 he was writing to his solicitor again, from his tower in the Jura, in almost hysterical terms about the delay in winding up his father's estate: 'Now, my dear Sir, if you have no regard for my interests I am willing to think you have for those of my wife – and I beg you to reflect what a situation would be hers if anything should happen to me, in the power of such a man as Sir William who *then* might put any construction he pleased, or abstract any papers he chose from the Executorship Trust – inextricable confusion!!!! Have the goodness, then, to settle these affairs as soon as may be – for I am so disgusted with the scenes of duplicity and wickedness constantly opening to my view – that I am seriously thinking of selling all my property in England and departing to N. South Wales ... '

'I wish to purchase land adjacent (to Glenthorne) with part of the remainder of the Entail Money. I shall have a battle to fight here, for Sir William consults the *taste* and convenience of my Successors rather than my taste and convenience but I hope if my titles are good to vanquish him.'

It is a sad picture of two good men being thoroughly nasty about each other and Nash Hilliard must have dreaded equally the sight of Sir William Cosway's neat, precise handwriting and the Reverend Walter Halliday's flamboyant scrawl. It is difficult to see what was to be done next but, only four days after Walter's last letter, fate settled the matter with surely excessive violence when William was killed in his fall from the Brighton coach.

Even though shock and concern for his sister were Walter's predominant emotions, he could not help but realise that he was now free to invest the money as he liked and he lost very little time in doing so. Strangely, in view of their mutual distrust, Walter was named, with one other friend, as executor of Sir William's will, but his sister, Elizabeth, a strong-minded lady, said she would prefer to manage her own affairs and Walter and the other executor lost no time in agreeing to this. No doubt Elizabeth was at least as capable as Walter at managing her affairs and it was probably owing to this lack of involvement that they kept up a good relationship and that Elizabeth and her children spent so much time with Walter and Katherine thereafter. Still, one suspects that Walter's main object was not to be involved in any affairs but his own.

From now on there was no more talk of buying estates in Dorset and Herefordshire, let alone Kent. Walter started to acquire land round Glenthorne. There had never been a traditional estate in that area so he had to set about buying land when and as he could, moulding it into some sort of whole. He managed to buy his estate in three main lots but, at times, the difficulties involved seemed insurmountable and it took him the rest of his life to acquire some parts, often small and peripheral, of what became the Glenthorne Estate of about 6000 acres.

It was a project which would have daunted the most sane and businesslike of men, but then, no sane and businesslike man would have entertained the idea in the first place. Certainly it seemed to call for very different qualities from those one attributes to the scholarly fancier of the picturesque. By settling in the wilds, Walter prepared seemingly endless difficulties for himself and one cannot help wondering if, as time went on, he found it all worthwhile and if there was ever enough mental peace for him to enjoy what he had already created and acquired.

In everything except his ideas on architecture and landscape Walter seems to have been thoroughly traditional: certainly his ideas of an estate and the duties and expectations of the owner thereof were quite conservative. Unfortunately, he chose to settle in a place where the natives had no such sense of tradition. They had never lived in a community under the sway of a resident landlord who laid down the law in exchange for some services and security. It was difficult enough to settle in a place remote, half-civilised, and poverty-stricken, but it was made much harder by the fact that the people there were used to independence. They were chronically short of money and ready to drive a hard bargain, but not to touch their forelocks and say 'thank you kindly, sir' for ever after. Exmoor in those days was probably too remote to be very much affected by politics but still, the whole temper of the age was for reform, and for people to have more voice in their own affairs. It was not a very good time to establish an old-fashioned paternalism where none had existed before and Walter must often have felt as though he was trying to turn a pack of foxes into house dogs.

Unlike the central area of Exmoor which had been a royal hunting forest until 1815, the high coastal strip had been settled and farmed after a fashion since at least the Middle Ages. The climate, the soil and the distance from any sort of centre had ensured that its inhabitants never really prospered, but a small and tenacious society had been in existence for a long time, and a tradition of agriculture had grown up.

Until the dissolution of the monasteries, most of Countisbury had belonged to the abbey of Forde and had been used as a vast sheep run with just enough people to keep an eye on them. The only variety in a rather lonely and monotonous life seemed to have come from its being on the coastal route that travellers and pilgrims took to Barnstaple and the quay at Bideford. After the dispossession of the monastery, parts of the land belonged, from time to time, to some of the big Devon landowners, but it had always formed the outlying parts of the estates and seems always to have been the first to be sold or handed on when extra money was needed for dowries or to provide for dependants.

Historically, it has always seemed rather forlorn. When Walter came on the scene, there were one or two men who owned a good deal of land and more who owned a very little indeed. Farming was in one of its frequent unprosperous states and everyone was, if possible, even shorter than usual of money. It seemed to be a buyer's market and, having acquired the land on which the house was built and the farm land immediately round it without too much difficulty, Walter may well have felt that he only had to play a waiting game to acquire more.

In fact, land did come up for sale fairly frequently but, apart from the often inflated hopes of the sellers, the legalities created countless difficulties. Legal documentation was very vague. Lawyers were a long way away, their services cost money and, in a limited and largely illiterate society, word of mouth, relationship and actual possession were what counted. When there were legal wills and titles, it became apparent that the land had been divided and sub-divided to provide for family interests so that many already small farms were divided into parts as small as sixteenths, and months went by and much money was spent in trying to track down the missing owner of, for example, five-sixteenths of a piece of woodland. The simpler documents are full of moieties divided and undivided, freehold and entailed on various lives.

Moreover, it had recently become even harder to trace all these heirs because this was the time of emigration when almost every family in this part of the world had at least one member who had gone to America, Australia or the West Indies. Even when they could be traced, correspondence was very slow, but often they seemed to have just disappeared. Years were spent in trying to acquire one farm in Oare. All the descendants who could be found were more than willing to sell, but one member of the family, last heard of in America, could not be traced. In the end, a sum of money, calculated to be equal to his portion was deposited with the family solicitor, and Walter was preparing to take uneasy possession when he himself died and the whole affair was apparently abandoned.

There were difficulties, too, in establishing the Lordship of the Manor. This was important to Walter because various rights, including the sporting ones, went with it, but it had been a matter of such insignificance for so long that it seemed almost impossible to establish and the usual apparently endless legal searches went on for years before the title was eventually made good.

Another set of problems arose from life bequests in kind and life annuities. There were literally 'sitting problems' like the widow Fry of Wilsham whose husband left her 'My big kitchen and the two chambers above and a garden for her life.' It must have been trying enough while the place was still in the family to have granny installed in the most useful part of the house, but an impossible situation when it came to letting the farm to an outside tenant or selling it. The only solution was to buy granny out, but this led not only to prolonged bargaining but to the problem of where to deposit the old person in a district where housing was very limited. Once or twice, Walter, as purchaser, had to undertake the payment of annuities for elderly relatives, but one Bale, who owned a relatively small piece of land, seems to have overdone things. Arrangements for the care of various dependants had been made when, as Walter says in an explosive letter to his agent: 'Bale has suddenly produced a blind daughter, which is really too much of a good thing.' Reading through various letters, one finds one's sympathies swinging from side to side. Everyone was trying to 'do' Walter, and he knew it, and he also knew that weakness at one point would lay him open to all sorts of subsequent abuses, but he was a kind man, and most willing, within reason, to improve the human situation as well as the natural one. From the other side, how was Bale to provide for his various dependants? It was little enough money he was getting for his bit of land and, once it was gone, so was one source of subsistence. It seems, too, that there was blindness in the family, for there is recorded another vignette of perhaps fifty years later when Blind Bale, the Fiddler, used to play country dances for the young ladies and their friends to dance to on the lawn of the big house

Through all these transactions there runs the same thread of a dire need for money. The purchase of the inn at Countisbury, the Blue Ball, and its attached buildings and land, caused such legal complications that it hardly seemed worthwhile, yet it had to be sold for it had come on the market only because of the bankruptcy of its owner. Most of the land that had come up for sale seems to have done so because the owners could no longer pay their mortgages and one man decided he must sell only when even his last wool clip was mortgaged in Ilfracombe. One seller, unable to bear the slow rate at which the sale was going through, asked, through the agent, if he could have some of the purchase money in advance. Walter refused because he 'regrets the complications caused by acceding to a previous such request.' Obviously, the local people must have thanked God for sending them a golden goose and they don't seem to have tried to kill it. Who shall blame them if they gave it an occasional squeeze just in case another egg dropped out?

At one time, two Smiths, father and son, had land for sale. As usual, there were mortgage troubles in the background, and the Smiths were not of a co-operative temperament. There is an exasperated letter from Walter's agent to him saying: 'Mr Gribble tells me that Smith junior will not do what he promised, and old Smith will not move, and many other things, to convince one (if any additional proof were necessary) that they are all a set of ...' In spite of the fact that father and son did not trust each other an inch, the Smiths were united in their desire to sell and a price was eventually agreed, but then a further complication arose: each of them claimed sole ownership and, once more, the lawyers had to set to work to establish which one of them should actually receive the money.

In spite of difficulties and delays and the pouring of money into various legal coffers, by 1850 Walter had nearly achieved his immediate objective: the ownership of the entire parish of Countisbury. There was only one farm still in other hands and, in May of that year, it seemed as though it was going to be possible to buy that too, when the agent reported: 'I saw Litson of Wilsham when he came to pay his Tithes, and he said he should not have spoken to me, but that he wished to know if you were desirous to have his Estate – *That he did not wish to sell it*, and should not unless he could get a good price for it. He said he should like to know in a few months, as he was about to come to some family arrangement as to giving up business and, in case he should not sell to you, he should divide the Estate into three parts between his three sons *and that then it would be too late to buy*. This is a very *cunning* way of putting the point but, nevertheless, from what dropt from you respecting his intention of retiring from business, it may be correct. I then told him that you were ready to take the estate at a fair calculation, and give him, over that, an annuity of £50 per annum. He said he did not care about selling, but that what he received, he should expect paid down and he should then build a house at Combes Foot. This certainly shows that *he had some* idea of selling and, however slight, such intention may be as by the above assertion he has *thought* of the subject. He said the property in Countisbury was worth £130 per annum, which I said was £30 more than its annual worth but, even taking it at his own rental, it would only, at 30 years purchase, be worth £4300. He then talked about not caring to sell, and I suppose, by way of a feeler, said he did not think £8000!!! was very much above its value. *My impression* is that he *wishes* to sell although he disclaims the idea and that he will not refuse a *tempting* offer, but I have now laid all that took place before you, and you will be able to judge for yourself. It certainly is the only estate in the parish that does not belong to you, but it strikes me that it must come one day, and without the enormous sacrifice that you would now have to make if you purchased it.' This sets the scene for a fascinating wrangle that went on for sixteen years. In the end, Walter got all that he wanted, but the honours, on the whole, went to the side of low cunning.

There are no records to be found of any more bargaining until June 1854 when Mr Riccard, the agent, writes again: 'Mr John Litson has kept his promise and made, through Messrs Pearse, Son and Crosse, an offer of his estate of Wilsham, but it strikes me that the sum asked is absurd. However, Messrs Pearse, Son and Crosse say that it is Mr Litson's *ultimatum* and that, if he does not sell now, he shall not do so at all at any price whatever.'

'He wants £6000 and the estate still to be subject to his Mother's Annuity of £30 for her Life or he will take £6500 in full for the estate and annuity.'

'I fancy this is a great deal of money myself, but it is asserted that the Farm is worth £150 per annum and that that, at 30 years' purchase, would be £4500, and that the woods and accommodation are well worth the extra £1500. You now have before you their views of the case, and you must decide for yourself – whether you will take it or offer them some other lower sum. From what dropt, however, it would seem he builds much on your anxiety to have the estate, and that thereby you will give more than its worth, and that some allusion was made to Mr Munday's calling on him and endeavouring to persuade him to exchange for Tebicote etc. etc.' (Tebicote was a holding at the far end of the next parish, and so of no interest at all to Walter!)

'That it would be a very advantageous purchase for you, there can be no doubt, and the ownership of it will give you possession of the entire parish. And it is worth something considerable on that account. I doubt much if you don't buy now whether you will ever have a chance again. These sort of people are queer tempered, and require considerable management.' Simple though John Litson's methods were, he seems to have shaken the agent's nerve.

The next letter in the bundle comes more than a year later, dated August 1855, and is in Walter's large and explosive writing, addressing his agent: 'I do not understand your letters about Litson's property – does he mean to include the Mill ...? I am willing to give £5000 for all the Wilsham and Mill Property, and pay the Annuity.' Here, things stuck again for some time until

Litson obviously felt that another push was needed. Walter's next letter is dated November 1856 and explains John Litson's new stratagem: 'There has been a report here that a Mr Travers, an eminent Grocer in the City, wishes to purchase Wilsham! Mr Munday has seen Litson, whose ultimatum is £4600 for himself, and £400 for his Mother's Annuity!!! This has caused me much trouble, but I have, after mature deliberation, decided that this would be playing the Bailey and Palfreman game again' (whatever that was?) 'and it is *so bad* that it would even be better to have a stranger at Wilsham than the present bad lot.' Then he descends from righteous indignation to low cunning and goes on: 'Admiral Moresby tells me that, should Mr Travers thus drive me into a corner, it would be inadvisable to make it clear thro' you as my legal adviser to him that I cannot approve of such conduct, and that he cannot expect any courtesy or even tolerance from me in respect to Hunting - Fishing - Shooting – which is his object in purchasing. It may be a Mare's Nest, at all events I shall remain firm to my original offer viz. £5000 for *all the Litson Interest* in Wilsham and Countisbury with the Mother's Annuity of £30.' This is followed by another letter in two days: 'I thank you very much for your letter and for your plain speaking. It is no doubt a matter of moment and I have thought much and consulted wiser men than myself – and I decide to abide by the terms of my last letter to you. In the first place *I do not* believe in Litson! nor will I take him or his farm at his own valuation. Wilsham lies in a corner by itself, and has nothing beyond its outring.' (This presumably refers to common rights.) 'It seems very improbable anyone should place himself in so false and unpleasant a position at such a sacrifice of Money! ... I offer £5000 including the Mill ...' This round seems definitely to have gone to Walter for, after his very brief appearance, Mr Travers is heard of no more.

The next batch of correspondence starts eighteen months later, in May 1858, with a letter from John Litson's solicitor to Walter's: 'Some time ago, you applied to us on behalf of the Revd W.S. Halliday (who indeed also wrote to us himself) to know the lowest price our client, Mr John Litson, would take for *Wilsham* – we did not then appear on the scene, nor did Mr Litson care at all about selling the property.'

'Such is still his disposition but, if Mr Halliday will make it worth his while, he will, by our advice, sell. Not long ago, Mr Halliday offered £4000 for the property and to pay the £30 a year charged thereon during Mrs Litson's life – this was not accepted, but we have advised Mr Litson that, if Mr Halliday will give him £4500 *and pay the annuity*, to sell.'

This sounds as though Litson's nerve was cracking, and that something was at last about to happen but Walter, either from temper or a false sense of having the upper hand, must have made a bad move because a month later there is another letter from Mr Litson's solicitor to Walter's: 'As we informed you in our former letter, Mr Litson has not the smallest desire to dispose of his Estate, and thanking Mr Halliday for his offer of £3500, we are instructed to decline it.'

The next documents, dated a mere eighteen months later, are a copy contract for the purchase of Wilsham for £5900 and a letter from Walter saying the solicitor may agree to anything on his behalf, and the deposit money is ready. More complications, however, cropped up because, ten days after the date of the draft contract, Walter writes to Riccard: 'I have naturally been very anxious to know what took place *really* in the late affair at Wilsham – and how far Lord Lovelace *did* or would go – and I thank you for explaining the matter, and I do not complain since it is worth more to me than anyone else.' Unfortunately, we do not have the explanation, and can only guess at what it was all about, but it seems to have had something to do with the mill, which was apparently excluded, after all, from the sale and, in any case, belonged to John Litson's brother, Gabriel. In a letter dated the following February, Walter says: 'I hope you and Mr Crosse will propose something about the Mill – before my Lord and his man Paramore come into the Market. I will give anything, within reason, but £1600 is out of the question.' The threat of Lord Lovelace was obviously to be taken more seriously than that of Mr Travers because he was a neighbouring landlord of eminence and, at a guess, looked on Walter much as Walter was prepared to regard the eminent grocer from London.

Meanwhile, it looked as though both sides were assuming that the sale of Wilsham was going through, because John Litson visited Walter to ask if he might stay on as a tenant and, at the same time, to try another little squeeze! Walter reported: 'He said also that his Mother had a House and Garden at Wilsham *which I might have* if I wanted – I said nothing – but I believe her husband left her £30 per annum with a house and garden as long as she lived – *or if she do not marry again*. Of course, the house and garden in this case reverts to me ultimately.'

Litson was told that he could stay on at a rent of £150 per annum which he seems to have accepted. The affair of his mother's cottage was left alone, and the contract was signed while the lawyers continued their searches and their correspondence in the preparation of the conveyance, and it was in the course of this that yet another complication arose. There was a piece of woodland that went with the mill, and it was assumed that that also belonged to Gabriel. But then it appeared that, after all, it belonged to John, so the question now was had he, or had he not, already sold it to Walter? Correspondence once more flowed, and legal opinion was once more asked. John Litson tried to solve the problem by hastily giving the land to Gabriel, but this was not allowed. Solicitors tried to solve it by persuading Gabriel to ask a reasonable price for the mill, but he insisted on the outrageous price of £1600, later reducing it to £1500. Legal opinion on the whole went against Walter who protested: 'Most certainly I should never think of claiming that which I never bought.' Friends advised him to have nothing to do with it for more than £1000. The mill was dilapidated and the wood was small, but it was the last little bit of Countisbury to be acquired. In November 1861 he weakened and bought widow Litson's cottage and garden for £40 and finally, in 1866, he bought the mill, the wood and the blacksmith's cottage from Gabriel Litson for £1150. At last, he owned the whole of the parish. One hopes that the landlord/tenant relationship at Wilsham was not too uncomfortable and that he found it all worthwhile.

There were, in fact, good practical reasons why, if one owned land on any scale at all, it was as well to own a whole parish. A hundred and fifty years ago each parish was responsible for its own administration and this included such things as road building and repairing, education and provision for the poor. There were other affairs, too, like common rights which were ancient, vague, but of great importance and which could best be solved by the people concerned. All these things were primarily the responsibility of the landowners within the parish and the more there were, the more difficult it was to come to any sort of decision. If one man owned the lot, the parishioners, no doubt, had to put up with despotism, benevolent or otherwise, but at least they were not at the mercy of warring despots and it did simplify matters in many ways.

On the other hand, the responsibility was great and if, like Walter, one decided to settle in a wild and Gothic landscape, one had to expect inhabitants to match. The relationship between Squire and parish was a paternal one and Walter obviously found his family difficult, especially as it was, so to speak, an adopted one, for he had bought his way in.

Like children in smaller families, they were ready enough to quarrel among themselves but quick to combine against authority if they thought it unreasonable. Walter also had to suffer from the suspicion and non–cooperation that reformers, improvers and do-gooders inevitably meet with, especially in small, isolated communities.

Theoretically, when he owned all the farms he could choose his own tenants but, in fact, the people who offered for them most readily were, naturally, those already in the immediate neighbourhood. In some ways this was as well, for the farming in each district is different and a farmer from one kind of land cannot necessarily cope with a different kind of husbandry, but it meant that the same cliques tended to band together and they were all well set in the good old ways. Certainly Walter had an agent and a bailiff to do a lot of his work for him but they, too, had to be directed and kept up to the mark. Leases were made out with full details of what the rotation of crops should be and how much lime and manure was to be carried and spread at what times, but there was continual trouble over those who omitted to fulfil these requirements. There were those who, knowing that they were about to quit, neglected fences and racked the land or those who ploughed up old grass pasture and those who were always in arrears. The excuses were many and had to be considered on their merits. One tenant, however, had the simplest and best excuse of all: 'He said he had not the money.'

No wonder exasperation breaks through from time to time. In 1833 Mr Riccard, the agent, wrote to Walter and to the bailiff, Charles Hooper, at the same time. To Walter he said: 'I strongly recommend that Combe, Trilleys, Hall and Yeanworthy be advertised to be let at once ... Such a course would make known the want of tenants in other parts of the County – any may bring some respectable parties into the neighbourhood.' To the bailiff he put it more tersely: 'I will do my best to get all the vacant Estates well let and, if I can do it, with men as far away from the neighbourhood of Countisbury, I will.' But the farms were not particularly tempting and he rarely seemed to succeed. The agent himself was, of course, a foreigner from South Molton, 23 miles away.

Twice a year, at Michaelmas and Lady Day, the parish 'Court' was held at the Blue Ball. It was not the Squire who actually presided here, but the agent and the bailiff. Here rents were paid, excuses were made, thanks were occasionally given for things like £5 for a dead horse, complaints and requests were heard and then a dinner was provided.

One of the most frequent causes of quarrels was to do with common rights. Originally, everyone who held any land at all in the parish had the right to unlimited pasture on the great tracts of unenclosed land and this, naturally, caused a great deal of trouble. When Walter owned the farms, he had the power to lay down the number of animals, ponies, sheep and cows which each tenant could pasture but, when all the animals were spread over the moorland and the narrow combes, it was extremely difficult to keep a check, even if all animals were, theoretically, marked. Of course, there were always objections to be met. In 1850, the agent reports: 'Mr Kent seems much inclined to take Hall, but he objects to the limit of 100 sheep on the common, stating that by sheep and wool the Rents are in that part of the world chiefly realised. I asked him £115 with the stint above named. If you will grant 300 sheep (and the more the common is stocked in reason, the better the herbage) will you leave it to me to try to get £120 per annum?' No doubt, if the 300 sheep were agreed on, another round of objections and requests would come from other tenants. When not quarrelling about numbers, there was another old custom which caused trouble. Each farmer used to take out men and dogs to drive other sheep from the neighbourhood of his own farm in order to keep it for his own sheep; this was generally done early or late, so as not to be seen. As ever, there was some basic sense in this; it was much more convenient to have your own sheep near at hand and sheep soon get 'leered', as they say on Exmoor, to their own patch but, of course, the temptation was always to drive the other animals as far as possible and squeeze them up in someone else's direction.

Gardens, too, were a fruitful source of friction. It was an old custom for farmers to allow old servants to make a garden in some part of the farm or on the edge of the common where ground seemed suitable. This, with somewhere to sleep around the farm or in a cottage, enabled the old people largely to support themselves without 'coming on the parish'. These gardens were often in odd corners, completely divorced from any house and, as the people got older, they tended to abandon them gradually, but it was often very difficult to tell just when they had been finally vacated. Sometimes, too, if an old servant had been allowed ground for a long time he claimed it for his own and, if there had been no agreement, no objection and possession for twenty years, the claim was legal and probably allowed common rights as well! This was a difficult problem for an incoming landlord!

In many places on the moor there are old banks partly enclosing smallish patches which mark the sites of these old gardens. There are, however, other banks marking larger enclosures all over the commons which are, at first, very puzzling, and one's mind wanders over the possibility of prehistoric settlements and evidence of more intense cultivation in former times, but they are not all so very old and are the remains of the old 'rye-breaches'. Apparently it was an undisputed custom for any commoner who felt the need to plough up a patch of common, generally of one or two acres, and enclose it temporarily to grow rye, potatoes or occasionally turnips. When the crop was taken in the hedge was 'thrown down' leaving only the foundation bank and cattle once more roamed freely, grazing and, of course, manuring. It must have been much in this way that early man first grew crops and indeed some nomads still do. Freshly cultivated earth will generally produce one or two good crops without fertilizer and, while ground remains, one can move on continually. This custom had almost completely died out by the beginning of the nineteenth century, but the local farmers were still fairly young in their understanding of fertilizing and crop-rotation compared with those in the more closely settled parts of the country and, after all, a rye-breach eased the pressure on one's own cultivated ground at no extra cost. There was also another good use to which the old breaches were occasionally put. If there were quarrels about boundaries and suspect encroachment on common ground, nearby breach-banks could often be claimed as old boundaries!

Even the smallest details were all to be handed up to Walter for consideration. Two of the farmers complained, when they came to pay their rents, that they were overrun with rabbits, so the keeper had to be ordered to deal with them but when he, in his turn, decided to deal with the rat and mouse population by means of poison, then, naturally, there was another outcry because of the danger to the dogs. There was also the question of the houses themselves. Most of them were more or less dilapidated when they were bought and they and the farm buildings obviously had to be made and kept weatherproof, but Walter wanted to go further and here opposition appeared again. When new tenants were moving in to one farm, he adjures the agent to impress on them that they are not to store corn, potatoes and fleeces in the parlour and they were to be sure to use the bodley. A bodley was one of the latest inventions in the way of a closed, mainly coal-burning, stove – the forerunner of the present day Agas and Rayburns. They were obviously a good idea then, as now, but many people found them suspect and difficult to manage and the agent is advised to impress on the tenants that the coal would cost not more than the wages of a servant to cut and cart peat for the old hearth fires. In another cottage, the tenant was perfectly willing to have a bodley and a good second-hand one was bought, but then it appeared that there was nowhere to put it as there was no back kitchen. There seemed to be no question of fitting it into the existing fireplace and it would have cost about £6 to build an extension to house it but only £3 to move the staircase, block a doorway and poke the stove-pipe through where the door had been. This would mean having two fires in one room but, as the tenant had no objection, naturally the cheaper way was chosen. As, until a few years ago, a spring always rose in wet weather by the back door to flow through this particular house and out of the front door, the tenant might well have been glad of two sources of heat in the kitchen.

Over and over again there is a paternal or headmasterly note in the correspondence which grates on us now and probably did on the tenants then. There are many variations in the agent's letters on: 'I told him it was a very poor return after all Mr Halliday's kindness' and 'I have given him a severe rating and told him he must pay his balance before July.' In 1854 there was obviously a tidiness drive and Mr Riccard reports: 'I also took occasion to call the attention of your several tenants to the benefit, as well as the comfort, to be derived from the keeping of their farmyards neat and clean – and also the condition of some of their fences and gates – and they have made a promise of amendment in these particulars ... and as to Ashton House, I do not well see how they are to avoid the filth you allude to. It is very bad certainly but, as the house now stands and the courtyard lies, I fear it is unavoidable. I will however look at it again the week after next when I come over. The house, with the exception of the back kitchen, is by no means unclean.'

Walter must by now have come to the conclusion that those happy and co-operative cottagers talked of by Uvedale Price and Robinson were mythical creatures; but he must also have realised that his chosen landscape, however picturesque, was as unco-operative as its inhabitants.

No doubt the local people shook their heads knowingly at this stranger's extravagant attempts to make their high, steep land more productive. His friends, the Knights, had already ploughed a fortune into the Forest of Exmoor. Still, Walter showed willing by keeping some of his land in hand and, although he made no startling innovations, he showed himself to be well-informed about current advances in farming.

The original Home Farm buildings were well designed and constructed in Robinson style and in the fields one can still trace the route of the old irrigation channels. This was a new idea which had recently been tried further into the moor and was probably a good one because, although Exmoor's rainfall is usually depressingly high, dry weather very soon affects the thin-soiled sloping fields. As horse-hoes and drills were invented they were ordered and, because the fields immediately surrounding Home Farm were exceptionally steep, mules were imported to supplement the horses. These were no doubt more popular than another of his imaginative innovations – wild boars to diversify the sport around Glenthorne.

In 1859 a report on *Farming in North Devon* was being prepared and one is struck by the authority and detailed knowledge with which he writes and how just, according to our present methods of farming the same land, his observations seem to be. It is true that wool is no more than a by-product now, whereas Walter exclaims proudly that 'The Exmoor Horn Wether is our chief *Stock-In-Trade*,' and that we have tractors to replace his 'Ten men besides boys and women occasionally – proportion of horses', but the method of farming here remains remarkably the same. The practical, reforming side of him must have felt justified in the outlay of time, energy and money when he concludes his report with: 'I see a great improvement all round, and a *desire* to improve ... but there is a want of Capital, Labour, Roads, Markets.'

It was fairly common practice for the Lady of the Manor to have special responsibility for the home farm dairy, but it is interesting to note that Katherine kept all the accounts and the notes for the farms that were in hand, as well as detailed household accounts. Her handwriting is as bold as Walter's but considerably easier to read and quite often copies of his correspondence are in her hand. It is interesting that although Walter was patron of the living of Oare, the half-yearly stipend of £26 always appears in her accounts. Again, it was fairly common practice for the ladies of the big house to run the school or, at least, to show some interest in it, but Katherine seems to have taken her duties with great seriousness. There are lists of furniture needed and of recommended books, which, contrary to some opinions of the period, did reach well beyond the catechism. Later, another school was started at Oare as well. Katherine's own books favour the poets and poetesses of the late eighteenth century, but her sensibilities were never allowed the get the upper hand and, in practice, she was a well-informed, kind and energetic helpmeet who probably greatly reinforced her husband's practical side.

When a stranger of any character or note comes into an isolated society, the consequent upsetting of the balance of things nearly always causes trouble. When two such people arrive, the situation gets serious! At one point in his Glenthorne career, Walter was caught up in one such affair. Strangely, but luckily for his future, although he was himself the later arrival, he was on the side of the natives. The climax came in the case of Halliday v. Palfreman, heard at Exeter in 1846 during the summer assizes. It makes romantic reading, but it is the romance of television serials rather than of literary lectures. It does, however, admirably illustrate the society of Countisbury in the early nineteenth century. The only account now in existence is that prepared by Walter's Counsel, so it is presumably as biased as it could well be without being positively untrue, but the facts must be substantially correct.

The case was heard in the summer of 1846, but this was the culmination of grievances that began twenty years earlier, a little before Walter even appeared in the district. In 1823 a certain John Palfreman came from the south side of the moor to Countisbury and began to practise as an apothecary. It is alleged that his affairs were embarrassed and that his qualifications were non-existent. However that might be, there cannot have been enough custom in the parish and its surroundings to disembarrass his affairs, or even to make him much of a living, so it must have been a godsend to him when he found he could make himself useful to the widow Slocombe of Hall Farm. Owing to a careless habit in her relations of falling over the cliff, Mrs Slocombe had become the owner not only of Hall Farm but of quite a lot of land in the parish and obviously management was difficult, so she must have been glad when John Palfreman gradually took charge of it for her. They lived as man and wife until 1827 when they married which, as Counsel for Walter says with spurious fair-mindedness, 'is a matter of little moment in reference to this case.' But, even before 1827, Palfreman had been very busy.

He began by enclosing about eighty acres of the adjoining common land. In order to keep the land within one fence, he diverted the parish road 'which now takes a circuitous route round the enclosure.' He must have been able to use a fair sum of Mrs Slocombe's ready money because he employed a small gang of navvies who had been working on Mr Knight's new projects in the middle of the moor. The other commoners could see well enough what was going on, but had no idea how to stop it. They gathered round the navvies, questioning and grumbling and, during the night, gaps regularly appeared in the day's work of banking and hedging, but it is said that they were too much afraid of Palfreman to do anything more positive. Three reasons were given for this fear; the first that, by his superior education, he could out-talk them, the second, that he was the nearest thing to a medical service in the neighbourhood, and the third, that if they objected, he threatened to make known the smuggling activities in which the entire parish was involved. As the banks were breached, they were built up again, taking in more, rather than less, ground until the acreage of the farm's 'in-ground' was nearly doubled but some corners, curiously, were left open. Later, it was discovered that this was so that the sheep could stray from the enclosure and thus keep up their common rights. In this way, things went on for some years with Palfreman determinedly outfacing the minor harassment and slow-burning resentment of his neighbours.

In 1830 the commoners came to a decision to divide and enclose the common and they held several meetings about it. Now of course the question of Palfreman's 'stolen' land came up, and they suggested that he should keep the land that he had already enclosed as his share and forego any more in the shareout. It was, from their point of view, a fairly handsome offer but naturally to accept it would be to admit guilt so he refused it, and finally the whole project was abandoned.

A few more years passed, but Walter, 'A Gentleman of unblemished character and conduct and who, from his Charitable Donations and unbounded kindness towards his poorer neighbours has gained the Esteem and Warm regards of all classes in his vicinity', according to his Counsel, had, by then, lived in Countisbury long enough to get to know what was going on and he decided to take issue for the common good. In 1840 Palfreman wrote a letter to the parish meeting admitting wrongfully enclosing ten acres and suggesting that similar proportions should be taken in by other landowners. This was most properly refused and in the winter of 1840, the first 'solicitors' letters' were exchanged. Several years passed and nothing at all was heard from John Palfreman's solicitors. This was puzzling at the time but it later transpired that the object was to allow twenty years to pass in the hopes of proving undisputed possession 'by custom'. At last, however, battle was joined and briefs were prepared. In case the plea of twenty years possession would not hold, as in fact it did not, Palfreman's defence rested on some ancient documents 'formerly in existence' proving that the land once belonged to Hall Farm and had 'gone back' to rough land. Various lumps, bumps and ridges were supposed to show old boundaries. Walter's solicitors, therefore, had to prove that these were merely the sites of old 'gardens' and 'rye-breaches' and, in order to do so, had to collect and interview all the most ancient inhabitants they could find. In spite of hard conditions, there seemed to be a surprising number of these – some of very great age – and it must have been a formidable task to collect their evidence, particularly if the enquirers did not speak the language. One witness is described as 'nearly ninety years of age and very deaf and infirm and speaks with imperfect recollection.' By the name of another, the solicitor has written: 'N.B. This witness is a very stupid old man and his memory fails him very much so that it will be well not to puzzle him.' It must have been quite a pantomime, but a difficult one to produce effectively.

In spite of unreliable witnesses and general obfuscation, the jury found in Walter's favour on half the many counts and awarded £200 damages. It was left to an arbitrator to settle the rest 'on the ground' and to award costs at his discretion. Finally, it was practically all settled in Walter's favour and Palfreman was ordered to pay costs. At this point, it became public knowledge that Hall Farm was, inevitably, mortgaged and that Palfreman was ruined.

Here any good story would stop, with the villain routed and the hero receiving universal thanks but, in fact, the sequel does dim the glory a little because, when the farm was put up for sale, Walter bought it. The disputed acres became his just as they would have become Palfreman's if only he had agreed not to demand more. It was no disadvantage for Walter to give up all claim to rough grazing for that farm on Countisbury Common because he already owned sufficient rights attached to land that he had bought elsewhere and he must have felt well rewarded for his chivalrous defence of local interests. When Palfreman himself died soon afterwards, he, in turn, must have departed this life feeling somewhat bitter. A large area of the common has never been enclosed and is now in the safe keeping of the National Trust. The original Hall Farm boundaries are still clearly visible but the road still follows the 'circuitous route' that Palfreman gave it.

A great number of these affairs were such as any landowner could expect to have to deal with. Whether cottages are gathered round a green, thatched and rose-hung, or spread here and there in the hollows and slits of a windswept landscape, most of the feelings and problems of the people inside them must be similar, but it is quite obvious that the mere physical nature of the Exmoor landscape made Walter's chosen job much harder. Countisbury Town consisted of a huddle of a farm and about five cottages round the church. One cottage had, not so long before, become the Blue Ball Inn and a school was built in the 1820s, but there was no natural meeting place and no shop – the bakehouse had fallen apart before the dissolution of the monasteries! The nearest markets of South Molton and Barnstaple were each about twenty miles away and could be reached only by muddy tracks that led over wild moors, up and down fearsome hills and round treacherous bogs. Communications of any sort were slow and difficult, and that much praised commodity, community spirit, cannot have been fostered easily. It was only to be expected that the people who survived there sometimes had their private methods of doing so. They must have been sturdy individualists and, understandably, more than ordinarily suspicious of anyone coming in, apparently to organise and enlighten them. The time that Walter might have spent contemplating nature must have been severely curtailed, but he may have felt recompensed when occasionally his agent was able to report: 'All your tenants seem content and doing well.' He seemed to have gained the trust and affection of a number of people who did not receive outsiders lightly and he had probably raised the standard of living a little in a neighbourhood that seemed to have less than its fair share of most things except wild and grand scenery.

Glenthorne must always have appeared remote and somewhat difficult of access and one wonders how the arch-romantic in Walter overcame the shrewder side of his character to enable him to settle there. However, the living conditions of the time would probably have made this choice of locality seem less impractical than it would today. Many parts of the country were still sparsely populated then, most roads were rough and the only means of transport apart from one's legs was the horse. Neither did domestic comfort depend upon shops, gas, electricity and machines but on numbers of people. If there were enough people to collect fuel and make fires, there was warmth; if there were enough people to look after the land and provide food, then one ate and there were generally enough people wanting employment in return for food and shelter to make this possible. In a remote part, there were fewer people but they were generally all the more desperate for work. Of course, money provided many more desirable things but, basically, big country houses were mutually supportive communities. They were not lonely either, for, added to the numbers already living there, guests came on leisurely visits, bringing their servants, who became the guests 'on the other side of the green baize door'. There was also the temper of the age. That time witnessed a great burst of optimism and a great sense of human power. With the winning of the long war and the increasing number of marvellous inventions, it seemed that nothing was impossible, and that everything that was just possible at the present time would become easy in the near future. The building of Glenthorne was quite a feat, but is nothing compared with what was done on Lundy Island not so very much later.

Walter's choice of where and how he lived must have been due as much to the ideas and ideals that were in the air at that time as to his own personality. What we loosely call Romanticism varied considerably as the century progressed. The Rousseauesque sort which started the return to nature and simplicity also celebrated freedom and the individual and was one of the major inspirations of the French Revolution – as well as of the romantic poets. The German variety, at least in the form in which it came to England, laid much more stress on sensibility and introspection, but it came too late to influence Walter. While, quite obviously, the French Revolution was not England's ideal in the early nineteenth century, social reform was very much in the air, if only to prevent a similar revolution. Certainly, whatever his original motives, Walter did succeed in living a simple life by current standards in beautiful, or rather, picturesque, surroundings and in benefiting the community. It is also interesting to note that this same devotion to the picturesque, combined with what we now call 'social caring', is held out as an ideal in Maria Edgeworth's novels and a little later in Susan Ferrier's, particularly *Destiny*.

However muddled or philosophically sound his motives were, Walter seemed always basically content with his chosen life. As time went on, he had a little less business on hand and his writing, though as vigorous as ever, covers more paper less legibly; in fact, an increasing amount of his correspondence seems to have been done by his capable wife. He was always noted for his particular brand of humour and this did not desert him. When archaeologists came to explore the area round Countisbury Church, he gave them something to think about by secreting a few Roman coins about the place, thus falsifying history for a little while. Indeed, he was so pleased with the success of this little joke that he took to burying small caches of money here and there for the pleasure of seeing if anyone found them, until Katherine took steps to limit his small change.

One day in January 1872 he caught a chill and took to his bed. In a very short time, and with no pain, he was dead. In her account book, Katherine enters for January 25th:

Countisbury Poor's Rate 6d. in £ a quarter: 8. 0. 9.

Bought hay for groom of Richard Keel: 6. 0. 0.

The next page is empty except for one entry:

Alas!! The Mournful Gap!! We have lost our Master –
Our Head – Our Friend – Our All in All! God help us!!!!

Then for six months the accounts go on as usual, except for extra items like:

	Black-edged paper and envelopes:	9s . 0d
and	Packing cord for my boxes. 20 yds:	2s . 1d

One might have expected that she would soon follow Walter to Oare Churchyard. After all, she was older than he was, but in fact, having tidied up estate affairs and given presents to all her staff, she moved to Clapham and spent the rest of her life in good works and the enjoyment of music, particularly Handel's, until her hundredth year, leaving Glenthorne and all its problems to the next generation.

THE INHERITORS

William

The problem of running Glenthorne became obvious as time went on but, when young William (always known as Halliday in the family) inherited, they were not immediately apparent. Walter might have been unbusinesslike compared with his relations, and his business letters certainly tended to read like rhetorical and exhortatory passages from his former sermons, but he had relentlessly followed his inspiration and, no doubt at a price, had created something which, though perhaps not unique, was certainly considered at the time to be rare. By the end of his life, the house and its surroundings had settled into an appearance of naturalness and inevitability, and it was this part of his achievement which caught the imagination most.

In many ways, the creation of the estate could be considered the greater achievement; not merely the acquisition of the land but the comparative peace, harmony and prosperity that now reigned. The farmhouses and buildings were in much better order than they had been when Walter bought them and they were supplied with more in the way of modern conveniences. The land itself was farmed in a better, or at least more regular way and here, too, some modern methods and aids had been introduced. This improvement was, no doubt, partly due to the watch being kept by Walter and his bailiff but, in some part, it was due to the knowledge that in real need there was somewhere to go for help. A little might also be due to the example set on Walter's own farm! Both the churches, at Oare and Countisbury, were in good repair and St John's, Countisbury, ruinous in the seventeenth century, had a new aisle to accommodate the larger population. The extensions at Oare were carried out in Walter's memory but, presumably, with what had been his money. There were two schools supplied with furniture and books to what, for the time, must have been a high standard. Jobs, of course, were created by the need for servants in the house and estate workers, but tradesmen from quite a wide area also benefited, judging by the receipted bills still extant for things like miles of iron hurdles for fencing round the estate. Payment, too, was prompt, thereby not so much relieving as creating a cash flow.

Benevolence may not have been Walter's aim in settling where he did, but he and Katherine were benevolent characters and a great deal of local good was done. Moreover, though sometimes against Walter's wishes, it had been done without dispossessing the original inhabitants so that there was a settled community and fair amount of goodwill. Owing, one assumes, mainly to Katherine's exertions, the accounts were all in exceptionally good order. Altogether, although to advanced thinkers it was an anachronism, it was a fair inheritance.

Sir William Cosway would have been greatly relieved that his hopes had been realised and that his only son, Halliday, had inherited Uncle Walter's possessions. He would, however, have been first incredulous and then horrified by subsequent events, for Halliday, by then a settled lawyer of forty-four, promptly moved into Glenthorne and made his home there, using Bilsington for what income it could provide. By the terms of Walter's will, it would have been impossible just to sell up Glenthorne and use the proceeds to finance and expand Bilsington, but Sir William would surely have found a way to push things a little in that direction. His son, however, made no attempt to do so. It seems that there was more of Uncle Walter in him than anyone could have suspected.

The difficulties of running Glenthorne gradually became apparent. The first was caused by the fact that in the 1870s there was yet another agricultural depression; the second was that there was virtually no liquid capital, for Halliday's inheritance was all in land; the third was his own character. If there had been more ready money he could have kept things going whatever sort of man he had been, short of being an inveterate and unlucky gambler. Conversely, if he had been more of a decisive character, more like his father in attention to business, or like his uncle in general interest in what was going on, he might have managed better, even with virtually no capital. As it was, although he was intelligent, educated and interested in current thinking, he seems to have had very little interest in either business or the economy of the country. Such ambitions as he had were towards public life, and that has always needed time and money more than anything else.

It is, in fact, difficult to tell just what sort of a man Halliday was;

compared with the rest of the family he remains in the shadows and has left very little paper behind him. There are a few letters, a few comments in other people's diaries, and a few memories from his daughters in old age but, even for the details of his education and career, one has to refer to official publications. One thing is certain, however, everything about him was correct. He was born in 1828, so he was only a year old when his grandfather, Simon Halliday, died, and six when his father was killed, so his early years were spent in a very feminine environment, but this was corrected, if that was necessary, when he was sent first to Winchester and then to Balliol College where he took his degree in 1850. After this he began to 'spread his wings' a little, and the first of his few remaining letters is to his mother asking for a temporary loan of £450 to pay the first instalment on his new yacht. It seems that, in one thing at least, he took after his father; he tended not to have quite enough money in hand for his immediate requirements. If it is the same yacht as the one that had its picture painted in 1868, it is a surprisingly imposing vessel for a young man who was not very rich. Its name was unexceptionable and uninteresting: *The Isis*.

Halliday cannot have had a great deal of immediate use for it because, before the end of 1850, he was off on the Victorian equivalent of the Grand Tour, which lasted for three years and took him through Switzerland to the Italian lakes, then to Frankfurt, Berlin, Dresden, Prague and Ratisbon, and on to Damascus and Baalbek. After that, he 'did' Italy thoroughly, climbing Etna in time to see the sunrise from its summit, then taking an excursion to Malta, via Syracuse, and, after that, spending a good deal of time in Rome and Florence before returning to England in 1852. The four letters which have accidentally survived from this period were written to one of his sisters and to his aunt, Katherine Halliday, which could account for their comparative stuffiness: he may have written in different terms to his friends and contemporaries. Still, one can only say that he seems to have had all the appropriate conventional reactions, which is a little disappointing. In Frankfurt, he tells Aunt Katherine that he was able to get some little insight into the mysteries of the Congress there, and was gratified to learn that 'the ne plus ultra of their ambition was to get their Constitution as like the English as possible', although he was afraid that time and bloodshed were inevitable and that 'these Germans carry their proverbial mysticism into their politics.' He found Berlin exceedingly handsome, and was sure that the famous street 'Unter den Linden' can scarcely have its equal in Europe but, as there were no antiquities in that wholly modern town, he soon passed on to Dresden for the Raphaels, Corregios and Carlo Dolces. The journey from Prague to Ratisbon was a thirty-seven hour endurance test through snow, deep in places, and over roads 'three times as rough as any in North Devon.' The few inhabitants of Bohemia were half-savage looking fellows but still he was able to talk to the courier in German and while away the time in political conversation.

His letter to his sister, Georgina, was written in Beirut and is rather tiresomely didactic in tone, even allowing for the fact that he is impressing his little sister. With all the wonders of Damascus, Baalbek, the Cedars of Lebanon and the orange flowers of Tripoli to draw on, he still manages to include rather a lot of the Bible and Milton. He sounds a little more human when he describes his excursion through the snow with six horses, baggage mules, and unenthusiastic Arabs to the Cedars of Lebanon and he was able to report that he had got a stick from one of the famous trees that had been so gigantic that it was difficult to reach a removable part. Presumably previous souvenir hunters had already had the lower branches anyway.

Throughout the journey he seems to have made good use of his time, observing the world in an educated, balanced and energetic way. One feels churlish when one gets impatient or bored, but one ends up with no idea of an individual at all. Perhaps he had suffered from being the white hope of the family. At all events he had little enough time to pursue his career or his pleasures for in just over a year's time, he was off on his travels again, this time accompanying his mother and sisters on a journey to Italy for the sake of Georgina's health. In spite of being the heir to a good inheritance from early childhood, he did pursue a career. In 1855 he took his M.A. and, in 1858, he was called to the bar in Lincoln's Inn. Then, in 1860, he married Maria Farquhar, the grand-daughter of Simon Halliday's old friend and relation, Sir Walter Farquhar. It seems likely that they had known each other for some time, as all the families involved knew each other well, but there is absolutely no information about this and no means of telling whether they fell in love, or whether the older generation got together and decided that, as it was high time that both of them were married, for Halliday was thirty-two and Maria apparently an established old maid of thirty-six, they might as well marry each other. Maria was the youngest of the family. Her older brothers and sisters had married well and she was used to moving in the 'best circles', but she had not managed, through many seasons, to make a good match and Halliday Cosway, a rising young lawyer, Lord of the Manor of Bilsington in Kent and heir to the Glenthorne estate on Exmoor, was by no means a bad proposition.

At all events, they duly married and settled in one of the new and fashionable parts of that fashionable and international resort, Torquay. Presumably work took them to Torquay, otherwise one wonders why it was chosen in preference to London or the Home Counties. It was not even very near to his future inheritance.

One is naturally most curious to know what he thought about his uncle's life-work on Exmoor. Did he approve of it? Had he the same sort of romantic convictions as Walter? And had he, and Maria for that matter, the temperament to love and cherish it? It is extraordinarily difficult to find the answers to any of these questions, but one thing does seem certain: he did not share his father's conviction of the superiority of Kent, for he never seems to have considered Bilsington as anything other than a source of income, such as it was. No doubt he had to prepare himself for living at Glenthorne as well as changing his name from Cosway to Halliday, and becoming Halliday Halliday when he did inherit, but a lot of his adult life was to pass before this happened. There seems no reason why he could not have spent the time managing and improving his father's cherished acquisition, even while practising law in London. One can only assume that he, too, had romantic leanings and feel sorry for his father, or happy for Walter, according to one's own temperament.

Maria

Though Halliday has left little of himself behind, there is much more to be learned of Maria, at least before her marriage, for she kept a journal and commonplace-book. Practically every member of the family kept a journal at some point, but they were journals of travels. In the last century, a little book in which to record one's impressions was as much a part of one's holiday equipment as a camera is now and, although publication was not necessarily one's aim, there was a semi-public intention in that one was prepared to delight or bore one's friends with it on one's return. Maria's journal did not come into this category. Almost daily for six years, from 1846 (when she was twenty) until 1852, she made some sort of entry of events and feelings while, beginning at the other end of the book, she wrote out long 'memorable passages' from her current reading. It is quite definitely a private journal written in a hasty, spidery scrawl that is quite as hard to read as Walter's florid script. Even the book itself emphasises privacy: it is a solid volume with hard marbled covers, a leather spine and a stout brass lock. It arouses all sorts of anticipatory interests and does indeed tell a lot, although, on the whole, it has to be admitted that it is very dull.

When he died, Sir Walter Farquhar must have had the comforting knowledge that he left his fortune in good hands. His son, Thomas, had settled down soberly and steadily in the banking house and divided his time between business at St James' and family life at Polesden Lacy. In due course he married Sybella Rockcliffe, the daughter of a clergyman, who bore him seven children in the next sixteen years and they, in their turn, were mostly highly satisfactory. The eldest, another Walter, became a partner in the bank and married Lady Mary Octavia, youngest daughter of the Duke of Beaufort; next came Caroline who married General the Honourable Charles Grey, a member of the Royal Household who became Secretary to Prince Albert and, later, to Queen Victoria. They naturally spent most of their time wherever the prince was, but their basic home was in Scotland while they had a town house in Eaton Square. The third child, Anne Sybella, married a young lawyer, George Clive, of Perrystone Court in Hampshire and Ballycroy in County Mayo. He was Assistant Poor Law Commissioner and a Police Magistrate in London and, for a while, Under Secretary for the Home Department, so they found it convenient to have a house in Surrey as well. The fourth child was a son, Trevor, who went into the army, and was, sadly, and probably needlessly, killed in India at the age of nineteen. Young, enthusiastic and inexperienced, it is said that he led a cavalry charge, was separated from his men and cut down while they stuck together prudently and were able to withdraw. The anniversary of his death is always marked in Maria's journal with some such phrase as 'sad and fateful day'.

The next child, Barberina, also died comparatively young. She married Mark Milbanks Esq., a gentleman from Thorpe Perrow, near Bedale in North Yorkshire, and died of consumption shortly after the birth of her third child and first son who did not long survive her. That left Harvie who married Louisa, third daughter of Lord Colbourne, and settled at Brackley House in Northamptonshire and, finally, Maria, who gradually assumed the profession of Mama's companion and universal aunt.

Sir Thomas died when Maria was ten so she became particularly her mother's child, but it was not by any means a confining life for later on, her mother travelled a great deal with Maria in attendance and, although she often went to spas for her health's sake, they were always fashionable enough for Maria to find suitable company. Most of the residents must have been too old or ailing to make life exciting but there was always the possibility of visits from younger and more robust relatives. In between, there was a choice of her relations' country houses to be visited in England, Scotland and Ireland and they all tended to converge on London for the season. There was leisure and money for travelling and as the railways were rapidly extending over Europe it became a much simpler business.

At first sight her diary reads rather like extracts from novels of high life: *The Queen's Ball, The Queen's Drawing Room, To the Opera in the Royal Box, To the Races, Dined Lord Beaumont's, pleasant time, Duchess of Leeds, Miss Fox, Sicilian Mr Panizzi, Lord and Lady Mounteagle, and to Lady Grey's after, Lord Advocate dined here, To Lady Palmerston's* ... All the ingredients for a good serial, preferably on colour television, are there but, as one carries on deciphering the entries, one realises that she has no interest in these occasions beyond recording that they happened. She was a very serious, not to say solemn, young lady who spent all the time she could claim as her own in solid reading, visiting exhibitions, having piano and singing lessons and going to small concerts dedicated to such works as the later Beethoven quartets. When she had no one else to chaperone her, she went with her much loved maid, Kent, who must have become one of the most cultured lady's maids in London, or else the most bored.

Conversations were described only if they had solid, noteworthy content. When visiting Scotland, she recorded one satisfactory dinner party at Lord Advocate Rutherford's where she had the great pleasure of sitting next to Professor Wilson and talking of

Goethe, Schiller and Coleridge in his youth; then, at another party back in London, she was able first to discuss Arnold's *Life* with Mr Stanley, then to move to a Mr Twistleton who talked of Goethe and revealed a preference for Wordsworth over Byron. There was a Mr Bezzi, too, who became a great friend. He had, she confided to her diary, been a kind mentor to her: 'He advised me to read Carlyle's translation (of Goethe) and goes with me to picture galleries.' Many dinner partners, armed with gentle gallantries, must have been put sadly off their stride by this young lady sitting in her white muslin, enquiring earnestly about the best translation of Goethe.

Even during the many journeys abroad with her mother, she kept fairly well to her routine This was the more easily done because these holidays were leisured affairs. The travelling Victorians thought in terms of months where we think in weeks and when she and Lady Farquhar went to Rome soon after Trevor's death they stayed for nineteen months. As soon as they reached their lodgings, a piano had to be hired for practice and amusement, then contact was made with friends or acquaintances already settled. After that, life fell into place with reading, writing and practice in the mornings, taking the waters if they were at a spa, socialising and going on parties of pleasure in the afternoons and dining out in the evenings. As they generally went to places with a fair number of English residents or visitors, it was relatively easy to keep to the established routine, although the Farquhars could not be accused of ignoring all but the English residents. On successive days while in Rome, Maria visited Princess Doris, Lady Mary Sartoria, Mme Potempkin and Lord Ward. Before she left Rome, she was reading and writing Italian with apparent ease.

There was a great deal of sociability; almost every day there was a sightseeing party, a ball or a dinner, but Maria still contrived to give an impression of great sobriety. In the six years of the journal there are only three entries that might count as frivolous. The first was during the carnival soon after their arrival in Rome when she writes: 'First day of Carnival, pouring rain, went in closed carriage to see the fun.' A year later, two days after her twenty-third birthday when her brother, Harvie, was staying with them, she records: 'Great fun at the Carnival, lovely day!' The only other sign of what many would consider normality in a girl is when she was presented at Court and records that she wore a white gown and a green train. A much more typical entry is one recorded on her journey to Rome: '18th October, Sunday, remained in Boulogne, went to English Church, rainy day. After Church, went to see the Crypt under the Cathedral, very curious sixth century, looked to me like the remains of a Byzantine Church, grotesque capitals and arabesques on walls painted with *pointed* arches which shows it must be after the sixth century.'

As one reads her comments and her 'memorable passages' at the other end of the book, one thing soon becomes apparent: she belonged firmly to the Romantic school of thought – or feeling – but it is also apparent that it is a romanticism that Walter would not have recognised. This is partly due to the passage of time; current ideas had changed a good deal between Walter's and Maria's formative years, but it must also be due to their different temperaments. Walter's romanticism was a sort of aesthetic trimming to his life. Maria's was a more inward philosophy. The commonplace-book starts with the Italian poets and Leigh Hunt's book on the subject is her guide. After that, she embarks on a long course of philosophy starting with the Stoics, going on to Plato and then jumping to Rousseau and Dugald Stuart's *Philosophy of the Human Mind*. After that, she goes back a little to Hobbes and then to Hume. The next few pages are devoted to W.S. Landor on *Poetry* from the *Edinburgh Review*, a critical magazine which she read with great attention, and to Aubrey de Vere's *Sketches of Greece* and then she dives into Goethe and there are 25 pages copied out, often in small writing, covering *Wilhelm Meister, the Conversations with Eckermann and the Life*. Finally there are 11 pages of turgid romanticism from a now obscure German book, *Titan*, by Jean-Paul, which she read in French. Here and there are a few verses of poetry, but the only poem which merits writing out in its lengthy entirety is *The Lyre's Lament* by Mrs Hemans!

There are two classes of literature which she takes very seriously, but which apparently did not exist for Walter. One was German romantic writing, and the other was the literature generally of the North. Goethe was born more than forty years before Walter and Schiller was publishing at the time of his birth, nor can he have been entirely ignorant of Germany, for his brother, George, was working in Cologne when he died, but culturally it did not affect him at all. His own outlook was based on the classics and the Bible. For modern literature he turned to England, France and

Italy. Maria, of course, being female, was not conditioned by a classical education, but for her generation Germany had become generally popular both for its philosophy and its spas. The same seemed to be true of other Northern literature. The new appreciation of simplicity that had started in the eighteenth century had brought with it the rediscovery and appreciation of ancient folk literature, notably the heroic sagas, whereas for Walter the Scottish ballads and Sir Walter Scott's novels represented the North.

In almost all Maria's reading it seems as if she was preoccupied with the relationship between the head and the heart, reason and feeling. If it came to a choice, she was unhesitatingly on the side of heart and feeling. On finishing Hume's essays she writes in the diary: 'Finished Hume and hate his principles, though admire his genius.' Utilitarianism found no favour with her and she copies out with approval a discussion of Tennyson's poems from the Westminster Review which advocates the heart's intuition as the only safe guide: 'Strange that a vision so clear and so far should miss the truth that the emotions are the only safe basis of a peace that cannot be moved, that a heart of sound, deep, warm emotions will create more light in and around itself – will more clearly record the love and wisdom of God's ways to man, though not united to the greatest powers of intellect ... we only ask that the intellect be unfolded in the atmosphere of the heart's affections and warm aspirations ... deprived of such guidance the intellect is not to be trusted.'

As one learns more of Maria, and as her character develops, one finds oneself wondering if such quotations were recorded as a warning to herself or, at least, as a goal, for her main pre-occupations were obviously intellectual and she seemed to have considerable difficulty with feeling. By contrast, Walter was very much a man of feeling although he might never have heard of Goethe.

A year later, when she was reading Aubrey de Vere's *Sketches of Greece*, she is still preoccupied with this distinction and copies out: 'The character of the South ... (is) unspiritual in its scope, appealing less to the heart than to the fancy, exposing everything to the understanding and, consequently, reserving little for a slowly apprehensive imagination.' And on a similar theme she quotes W.S. Landor from the *Edinburgh Review*: 'The difference between ancient and modern poetry is in some means analogous to that between the landscape of the South and North ... the Southern landscape is more beautiful to the senses and lends itself more easily to art: the Northern makes a more touching appeal to the imagination and lives more in the affections.' From this one realises that one must not confuse 'heart' with 'sensuality', that 'fancy' is different from and inferior to 'imagination' and that the feeling under consideration is on a high spiritual plane.

To many people this comparatively new philosophy was welcome because it seemed to suggest that one was all right if one just felt and did not bother to think, but Maria expected to have to work harder. She believed with Albano, Jean-Paul's hero of *Titan*, that one should have 'L'ame ardente' continuously alive to all impressions from nature and also with Goethe's *Wilhelm Meister* that 'men are so inclined to content themselves with what is commonest; the spirit, the senses so easily grown dead to the impressions of the beautiful and perfect that everyone should study, by all methods, to arouse in his mind the faculty of feeling these things.' Again, 'Without earnestness, there is nothing to be done in life.' In fact, by the time one has read through all the important quotations one realises with something of a shock that this is a very exclusive philosophy and suitable only for those with leisure and freedom from material worries. It may not, theoretically, be based on 'the greatest powers of intellect' but the tireless cultivation of such exquisite sensibility must have been a full time job. Neither Maria's grandfather nor Simon Halliday nor William Cosway could have spared the time. The way of life that their money provided was needed to make it possible for their heirs.

Nature, of course, played an important part in the cultivation of the soul and it was bound to be obtrusively important to anyone who was proposing to live at Glenthorne. Maria had plenty of opportunity to visit places celebrated for their beauty and she did so with proper assiduity, but it comes as something of a surprise to realise that her emotions, or at least her expression of them, were the most lukewarm of all her journalising relations. She never launches into descriptions of any length nor does she differentiate between the sublime, the picturesque and the beautiful as the previous generation of travellers did. She is content with a vocabulary of 'pretty', 'lovely' and 'beautiful' and, occasionally, 'exquisite'. The scenery round Lyons was 'pretty' as

91

was that between Avignon and Aix, even though the olives were stunted. The situation of their hotel in Cannes was 'exquisite' and so was Nice, while Monaco was 'very lovely'. It is a different vocabulary and a more careless one.

The things she records with more care are historical and factual. On leaving Lyons, she mentions that, on skirting the Rhône, they saw fine old castles, but space is given to recording that they passed the place 'from whence the Hermitage wine is brought, it is said to have been brought from Shiraz, Persia, 300 acres of it alone'. Passing through Orange, she launches into its history and its connections with England and, though she does state that Mentone and its surroundings are 'very lovely', she seems to be finally convinced of this because Ariosto in *Orlando Furioso* alludes to its rich vegetation. Whenever she was in the country she went for walks, but one suspects this was for fresh air and exercise and a change from sociability: a medical rather than a mystical experience.

Like Walter, she enjoyed pictures and wherever she was she visited galleries, exhibitions, studios and, when possible, private collections of pictures and sculpture. She writes more fully about the pictures and painters and her feelings about them, than about anything else. She is obviously in earnest, even though, unlike many Victorian young ladies, she never had drawing and painting lessons. Edward Lear was one of her friends and she saw him regularly in London and in Rome, but there was never any suggestion of lessons, even though he did occasionally give instruction – at least to Queen Victoria! To Maria he was primarily a musician and they enjoyed playing and singing together, although she did say that he did everything well.

After a visit to the picture gallery in Frankfurt, she lists some of the pictures which impressed her most, such as Overbeck's *Religion ministering to the Arts*, beautiful cartoons by Steinle of the *Sermon on the Mount*, *The Wise and Foolish Virgins* by Schadon, Becker's *Shepherd struck by Lightning*, *A flock of sheep* by Robell, *The Good Samaritan* by Julius Schnon von Carlsfeld ... Looking through the diary and comparing this list with others one realises that she rarely mentions a landscape, and indeed Robell's flock of sheep is the only non-human subject worthy of the list. Moreover, when she mentions why she likes a picture, it is usually because of its feeling. As with literature, the more heart there is, the better it must be.

Walter admired, and collected, pictures where nature was paramount. Claude, Poussin, and Salvator Rosa were the great masters in his estimation, and in almost all of their pictures the figures and buildings in the landscape are so small that they serve only to underline the vastness of the natural scene. They do not portray feeling, but they provoke it, and by the scale as well as by the subject, the feeling is generally one of awe.

For Maria, pictures of people were the most interesting and, as the people grew in importance, they tended to fill the space, so, both in reality and in feeling, there was room for nature only around the edges. She also liked pictures of people in dramatic circumstances. It was not the figures she admired, but the feelings they portrayed. It was always the expression, the feeling, the heart, she remarked upon, and the lighting, colour and background all had to contribute to this. It was also a much more explicit art in that it sought to portray people reacting in certain circumstances with such immediacy that one experienced their feeling sympathetically. In some ways, too, it was a literary art, or at least illustrative. Almost all the pictures she mentions are of reasonably well-known stories or events and, in recognising the particular scene, one is reminded of the rest of the story and, presumably, one's feelings are thereby magnified. She describes Steinle's drawing of the *Merchant of Venice* as 'embodying the whole play' but, to appreciate this, one would have to know the whole play!

Walter, being rich and independent, could go round Europe buying the pictures that he fancied. Maria, being a dependent female, could only admire and encourage. While she was staying in Germany, she had the good fortune to be introduced to two artists in their studios. One was Frederick Leighton, later to become Lord Leighton, the other was Steinle, whose pictures she had already mentioned a few times with admiration. It is most probable that the pleasure was all on her side for she had already developed the manner of a patroness, if her diary is anything to go by. 'Young Leighton', as she calls him (he was four years younger than her) was, she felt, 'quite an enfant de la nature, very clever in all ways.' He would, she was sure, be a great painter some day. He gave her a small engraving of a dead knight on a bier, but it may have been in gratitude at her departure.

She met Steinle in a picture gallery and boldly asked to see his studios. Having received his permission, she went the next day and then again very soon after. She felt so much in sympathy with him that she made a list of possible subjects for him in her diary. One is embarrassed for her, and sorry for Steinle, if indeed she did take them to him, but they illustrate admirably what, for her, constituted a really good picture. She starts off with 'The destroying angel leaning from Heaven presents to David three arrows from which to choose, war, pestilence, or famine, in the Heures d'Anne de Bretagne beautifully executed. The destroying angel sent to chastise David is beheld standing between Heaven and Earth with his sword stretched over Jerusalem to destroy it – none of the great masters have treated this – Rembrandt might have given us the terrible and glorious angel standing like a shadow in the midst of his own intense irradiation. David fallen on his face, and the sons of Amon hiding themselves by their rude threshing floor.' Further down the page, she has moved to ancient Rome: 'After the burning of Rome, Nero threw upon the Christians the accusation of burning the city. Peter, besought by his friends, left Rome. Two miles from the gate on the Appian Way he was met by a vision of the Saviour going towards the city. Struck with wonder, he exclaims: "Lord, whither goest thou?" (Domine Quo Vadis?) Looking upon him with a mild sadness, the Saviour replied: "I go to Rome to be crucified a second time." Peter, taking this for a sign that he was to submit to his suffering, returned to the city. Michelangelo's famous statue in Santa Maria Sofia Muricina, Rome, represents Christ as he appeared to Peter and Church built on the spot, Domine Quo Vadis. A fine picture the two figures would make, placed in such grand and dramatic contrast. Christ in his serene Majesty, and radiant with all the glory of beatitude, yet with an expression of gentle reproach, the Apostle at his feet, arrested in flight, amazed, and yet filled with trembling joy, the background the wide campagna and towering walls of Imperial Rome. These very grand materials. There are more similar ideas and one can only be grateful that her suggestions are almost always biblical: it gives one something of a start. Even so, if Maria had been an artist, her viewers would have had to rely heavily on their catalogue notes.

However tiresome Maria's enthusiasm might have been to some, it was real and lasting and, in 1855, she produced a *Biographical Catalogue of the Principal Italian Painters with a Table of the Contemporary Schools of Italy*. According to the title page, it was designed as a *Hand Book to the Picture Gallery* and although,

'It is difficult to see the track that winds down from the barren moorland through three miles of hairpin bends to the house lying in a sort of composed lunacy at the bottom.'

Sir Walter Farquhar, Bart. Portrait by Reynolds.

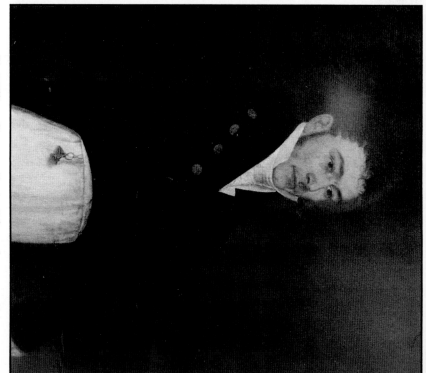

Sir William Cosway. Portrait by unknown artist.

Old print of Lynmouth showing villa built by Walter halfway up the cliff.

*The view from the Decision Stone – artist's impression drawn
four years after building had started.*

The Picturesque – early print of Watersmeet by W. Spreat.

The Picturesque – early print of Glenthorne by G. Rowe.

Design for a Gate Lodge from P.F. Robinson's Rural Architecture (1822).

Design for a Bailiff's House from P. F. Robinson's Rural Architecture *(1822).*

Glenthorne in 1839 – watercolour by unknown artist.

Dining room with some of the original furniture (1970s).

The tapestry room (1970s) showing original Aubusson tapestries illustrating La Fontaine's Fables.

The tapestry room window (1890s) looking out on the Stone Pine and the Bristol Channel.

The library in the 1970s showing Walter's books.

The library mantelpiece.

The Lodge – showing P.F. Robinson's influence.

Entrance to the Lodge showing Boar's Head gateposts.

Watersmeet at the turn of the century.

Portrait of the oak bed by Sir Alfred Munnings.

Mrs Katherine Halliday, aged 66, by Joseph Severn.

The Reverend Walter Stevenson Halliday, aged 62, by Joseph Severn.

'Lord of the Manor of Countisbury' (about 1870).

Farmer Ash and his wife, outside Combe Farm.

William Halliday Halliday with Helen Sybella (standing) and Constance Caroline.

William Halliday Halliday as High Sheriff of Devon 1882.

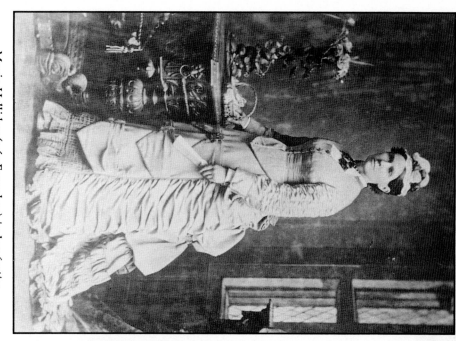

Maria Halliday (née Farquhar) in her forties.

Marion Cosway.

'This part is ours; nature may begin beyond this point' – showing the new billiard room.

*The billiard room in the 1970s showing the carved fireplace
and the unstructural beams.*

Helen Sybella, Constance, Lucy and Isobel Cosway admiring the rose garden.

The Misses Cosway again in Middlemead, showing the conservatory.

Lady Sybella Farquhar not long before her European tour.

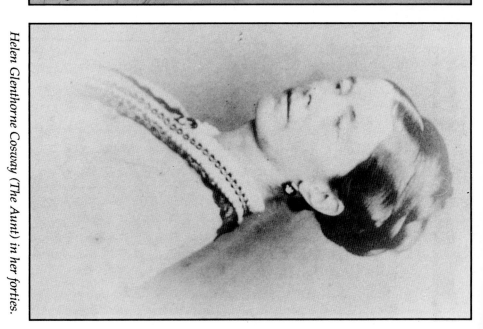

Helen Glenthorne Cosway (The Aunt) in her forties.

Lady Bayford, neé Lucy Sophia Cosway in middle age.

Constance Halliday and The Aunt, Helen Glenthorne, in old age.

Constance Halliday and Helen Sybella Cosway in old age.

'It still sits composedly on its ledge.'

conventionally, it was attributed on the title page to *A Lady*, the short foreword is written in Maria's name. It is a painstaking work of reference that must have taken hours of research.

Faced with so many references to the paramount importance of heart, feeling and enthusiasm, and knowing that Maria never missed going to church unless she could not possibly help it, one is almost reluctant to launch into her ideas on religion, fearing turgid pantheism, but, surprisingly, it seems this was no subject for enthusiasm. While in Edinburgh she went to a service at St Paul's and, though she thought the Scottish form of service incoherent, she found it well worthwhile because the Bishop preached 'a perfect sermon, so sound and practical.' When, later on, she was back in London and went to hear the poet Robert Montgomery preach, she was not much impressed, for he had 'wonderful eloquence, but not much matter.' Turning to the back of the book, one finds a note of Lord Campbell's letter to Miss Selon, warning her about the perils of giving way to religious impulses and Lord Erskine's remark that some of the darkest prejudices of men arise from the most honourable principles.

She went to church if she possibly could, wherever she was, and naturally she went to the English Church if there was one, but she does not seem to have belonged to that section of the religious English community that felt it would be contaminated by going near a Roman Catholic, nor does she ever sneer at other people's religious habits. On her first Easter in Rome, she went on Maundy Thursday to St Peter's to the exposition of the relics, and then to the feet-washing at night. On Good Friday, she went 'to our own Church and took Sacrament, then to St Peter's in the afternoon to see the Pope visit the relics.' On Easter Sunday, although it was rather stormy and cold, she was out watching the procession. She may well have been taking a tourist's interest, but it was a serious interest, and this attitude is borne out by the quotations at the end of the journal where she records Dugald Stuart defending various forms of religion as different disguises for workings of the same nature, and quotes her friend, F.D. Maurice who had published *The Kingdom of Christ* in 1838 pleading for unity and *The Religions of the World* in 1847. She copies out long discussions by W.S. Landor and Aubrey de Vere about the Greek attitude to Pantheism. Altogether there is an easy impartiality about this which one did not expect.

Her journal gives the impression of a dispassionate, enquiring intellect by many more of her chosen passages. 'New facts and ideas,' she quotes, 'are important, not merely for themselves, but in how we relate them to each other, and to what we already know.' The overall impression is one of a serious, solidly enquiring mind, with little humour or, indeed, imagination. Owing to the ideas then prevalent, she was intellectually convinced of the superiority of heart over intellect; she could see the necessity for spontaneous feeling but, as she had to use her reason to license her feeling, the spontaneity became lost. She believed in spiritual flight, but had to 'flap her wings' very hard indeed to rise an inch or two off the ground.

On the one recorded occasion when she did take flight and fell in love, it was, for some undisclosed reason, a disaster. In October 1849 she was staying with her mother at her sister, Caroline Grey's, house. Charles Grey had just been appointed Secretary to Prince Albert which had caused a certain amount of family gratification. Maria had just started to read Hume and everything sounded normal. She begins one entry in her diary: 'Thought of going to Chillingham, but gave it up. Mama not feeling inclined, very windy ... '; then suddenly she breaks into Italian which translates as: 'My thoughts today are far away and are my very own ... who knows the pleasure it would give me to hear you speaking, my very dear friend ... all the time my heart is with you ... It is a year today since we were together ... Your beautiful soul is always with me ... It seems to me that your personality has no flaws ...when I think of the richness of your soul and how you are endowed with every natural gift ... it seems to me that the time of our separation is long.' The effusion is dated exactly ' 1/4 - 2, Oct. 30th 1849.' Coming after so many pages of contained propriety, it is a shock. One shuffles quickly back through the pages to search for clues in the previous year but, among all the masculine names casually mentioned, there are no hints. Nor can one guess why she wrote in Italian: was the object of her affections Italian, or did she feel it was a more romantic language, or was it for greater secrecy? It is understandable that love should bite hard on such a serious character but even so a year is a long time to keep such a passion alive, with all the diversions of a very full social life and without any meeting on which to feed it. Even more worrying, however, is the nature of the infatuation. Even in an age when love, at least before marriage, was expected to be impossibly idealistic, one worries about an affection which seems to be based entirely on a beautiful soul enriched by every natural gift. Here indeed is the romantic hero! The next day she is still miserable enough to record: 'Very windy day – took a walk in kitchen garden by self, many thoughts came into my mind of the past and future', but the entries that follow are all normal, recording donkey rides, visits, the progress through Hume's essays, hating his principles of 'deriving all things from Utility', a session arranging books with Caroline, and a Public Thanksgiving for the abatement of the cholera.

Then, a month later, there is a pressed leaf between the pages and another unusually long entry: 'Fine, frosty day, clear, dry air, took a walk, and many thoughts came into my mind, mostly melancholy, thought at 2 o'clock on – how strange that simple things sometimes have power to comfort as, while my melancholy thoughts were coursing one another through my mind, and many things made me feel very unhappy as to the future, my eyes rested all of a sudden on a tree, the sole one which was not denuded of leaves, the sere and yellow leaf still remained faithful to the tree, it seemed to bend towards me and whisper, do not despair but *hope*, see how many storms and blasts I have encountered and yet I have withstood them all, energy of mind belongs to man, use that energy, bemoan not fate when it comes, but resign yourself, when my time shall come, I shall fall to the earth like my brothers, meanwhile I do not pass my life in bemoaning what is inevitable. I trust the best and, when evil comes, I resign myself to my fate. Tree, thou didst comfort me and I thank thee for it, this leaf all frosty I picked up and shall cherish as soothing my remembrance.' It is dreadful fustian stuff, but it is interesting to note that the romantic convention of the bond between man and nature is strong enough for nature to be pressed into service here. It is the only time that Maria records herself as in sympathy with nature. Whatever one thinks about her literary style, however, the poor girl was miserable enough and, if she really did take this lesson of stoicism to heart, it is very sad indeed.

We never discover who the object of her affections was or whether he was unsuitable or a jilt, or whether the passion was all on her side, but nothing came of it and she suffered for a long time. In the following February, she was staying with her sister, Anne Sybella, and brother-in-law, George, who were worried enough to take her aside separately and talk to her, but with no good results. On 6 March she writes: 'Birthday, 25! did not pass it very happily for I felt very ill and out of spirits.' And the next day, the doctor was sent for. By the next week, however, she was exerting herself and gradually the whole affair fades. One wonders, though, whether this was why she seemed to become more of a bluestocking and why she married so late, and one does so hope that she found some evidence of a beautiful soul in William Halliday Cosway that is not immediately apparent to posterity.

It is not nearly so easy to like Maria as the other people in this history. She seems to have been solemn and priggish and, even allowing for the strain of long exposures in Victorian photography, her pictures show her looking like a melancholy horse, but it seems as though she suffered principally from being born at the wrong time. If she had been born at the beginning of the twentieth century, instead of the nineteenth, she could have had a sound university education, indulging her desire for knowledge and understanding and exercising what was surely a good, wide-ranging intellect without seeming singular. In like-minded company, she might even have learned to relax a little!

After all, what really interests one about Halliday and Maria is how they were going to fit into life at Walter's adored Glenthorne, and what they were to make of it. Without waiting for dead men's shoes, they must have had their future there steadily in mind. Were they looking forward to it, and how did they envisage their future? Was Maria expecting to cultivate her sensibility in an ideal setting, or was she going to miss the society of Torquay after living there for twelve years? And what was Halliday going to do? Did he envisage himself like his father, who could be only a dim memory to him, a reforming and improving landlord, or was he looking forward to a more public life? Glenthorne would apparently give him the leisure for this, but too much isolation to make it easy. However well prepared they were, the change must have been great, for Torquay had much more to offer socially: with the extension of the railway, it was comparatively accessible from London, and it was also a favoured place for refugees from the continued political troubles across the Channel, so an interesting, cultivated and cosmopolitan society had collected there. As it had become fashionable, it had grown and it was undeniably beautiful. There was also a good harbour for Halliday's yacht, as well as beautiful country for carriage drives and picnics.

At all events, in 1872, when they were both in their forties, they and their four little girls took possession of their promised land, changing their surname and arms to Halliday, in accordance with Simon's will, so that Halliday became, rather awkwardly William Halliday Halliday. Once again, Glenthorne was to have no direct male heir. Maria had four children with all possible speed between 1860 and 1865 but they were all girls, and by the time the youngest was born she was forty-one and no more could reasonably be expected. However, that was a problem for the future. It was a sizeable household, because Halliday's mother was still alive and she spent a good deal of time with Halliday and Maria, together with her two remaining daughters. Of Halliday's four sisters who used to spend a rather hurly-burly youth, riding round Exmoor with the students from Selworthy, the older two, Eliza Sophia and Georgina, had died of consumption when they were just grown up, and the younger two, Helen and Marion, had shown no disposition to marry. When their mother died in 1876, although they kept on the house built by their father in Cowes, they virtually lived at Glenthorne. Some indication of the general attitude to their inheritance is given in a letter from one of Maria's old friends, Benjamin Jowett, the celebrated Master of Balliol: 'I am very much pleased to know that you are now settled at Glenthorne, which by accident I did not know of until a few weeks ago. You have got one of the most beautiful possessions in England, I dare say you will know how to improve it if you live there a few years. I hope, among other things, that it may lead to the realisation of W.H.C.'s political aspirations.'

One can only assume that Halliday's political aspirations were, like those of his father, to enter Parliament. If so, they were, like his father's, never realised. He was a Magistrate for both Devon and Somerset and Chairman of quarter sessions for Devon. He also had the honour of being High Sheriff of Devon for the year 1882-3 and was photographed in uniform holding a handsome feathered hat, but he reached no wider field of influence. Nor does he seem to have had any noticeable impact on the estate. The 1870s were a bad time for agriculture. There had been a slump after the Napoleonic Wars when Walter was spreading his wings, but a return to peace and domestic affairs had helped

England to put her house in order and, about the middle of the century, Walter was able to view his new estate as a going concern. By the time of his death, however, another agricultural depression had arrived. Halliday was more dependent than Walter on income from the estate just when the tenants began to find it more than usually difficult to produce their rents. He does not seem, either, to have been particularly interested in the actual farming or the tenants themselves. There are no schemes for better husbandry and no record of schemes such as his own father's loans to poor families to help them to emigrate, even though, not so very far away, Canon Girdlestone was helping poor people of the West Country to resettle either overseas or in the more prosperous North of England. Walter was known to the family, and particularly to Halliday's father, as unbusinesslike, but he was keenly interested and, although no doubt money was an essential ingredient in his methods, he obtained results. Judging by odd letters still in existence, Halliday's agent would have been glad of a little more interest but Halliday, no doubt, believed it was no good keeping a dog and barking himself, and that it was the agent's and bailiff's business to run the estate and hand over the money while he concentrated on other things.

He had a keen interest in politics, and references in surviving letters show that he discussed them seriously with his friends. It is interesting to note in passing that he attributed Disraeli's political overthrow to the influence of his novels. 'As far as the idea of him which has become prevalent goes beyond the truth,' he writes, 'he has his own novels to blame for it. An inference from a man's fictions to his politics is very precarious and liable itself to be not a little fictitious.' Halliday also had something of a reputation for scholarship, which would have recommended him to Maria. He bought the solider new publications as they came out, and his bookplate is in such books as Emmanuel Deutch's *Literary background to Christianity*, Renan's *Livre de Job* and Drummond's *Philo-Judaeus or the Jewish-Alexandrian Philosophy*. Like Maria, he had an interest in Carlyle and bought Froude's *Thomas Carlyle in London*. He read John Stuart Mill, and bought a good deal of history by modern writers. He kept up his classics, too, for there is a letter from Lord Lytton to Maria, dating from before they inherited Glenthorne, accepting an invitation to dinner and saying: 'If Pindar is to be the theme of our talk, I shall be delighted to *listen* to Halliday' and, in another, he is full of praise for his powers of translation: 'The verse taken from Anacreon is quite charming and is full of the inimitable grace of the original. I like, too, Mr Cosway's translation from Pindar better than that in the Book – it is bolder and simpler.' Both Maria's and Halliday's capabilities were admirable but perhaps not the best qualifications for running an estate in difficult country at a difficult time. To Halliday it seems the estate was a background, an income and an enhancement of consequence, to enable him to pursue his own interests.

In and around the house, there were a few alterations, some no doubt Maria's responsibility, but some, notably the billiard room, were Halliday's. The billiard room replaced the conservatory and was built in the same architectural style as the rest of the house but, inside, it is heavy and unconvincingly baronial. Its fireplace has an impressive, locally carved oak surround but the varnished beams in its open roof are noticeably unstructural. Originally it had a porridge coloured wallpaper with a scalloped border as a background to an assorted collection of armour and weapons. The result was an uncomfortable cross between a baronial hall and a Methodist Chapel, which betrayed a lamentable uncertainty of taste. Elsewhere inside the house a little heavy mahogany crept in to replace ageing satinwood, but the other changes were all outside.

In place of Walter's lawns which sloped gently and unadorned to the cliff edge, a croquet lawn was laid out at the side of the house and then, at a lower level, a formal rose garden stretched its geometric beds between the foot of the terrace and the 'sea-border'. It was always, and still is, a continual struggle to keep a reasonable level of civilised human life going at Glenthorne in the face of opposing natural forces, but Walter had arranged his surroundings to give an illusion of being at one with nature. Maria's and Halliday's surroundings declared much more firmly: 'This part is ours; nature may begin beyond this point.' It emphasised the battle too because the rose garden was, and is, very hard work and, until the questionable blessing of myxomatosis nearly wiped out the rabbits, it had to be almost entirely obscured from view by protective fine-mesh wire netting. Maria had no intention of emulating Jane Austen's Mrs Elton and abandoning her books and her music when she married. She was even totally untroubled by the responsibility of her children and her servants, because her sister-in-law, Helen, diminutive in size, was a tower of strength: she liked managing and was good at it. Maria kept up a voluminous correspondence with her many scholarly and literary friends, and would have had a continuous stream of them visiting in house parties that would have been like residential salons. Tucked at the back of drawers, a handful of letters has survived, most of them from well-known literary figures of the time. Many of them answer serious queries on philosophical and religious subjects and send effusive thanks for photographs of beautiful Glenthorne, for baskets of fruit, and hampers of game, and for kind invitations to come and stay, but regret the inability to allow themselves that great privilege owing to lack of time and opportunity. Some contain apologies for not having answered *all* Maria's interesting communications earlier. It is probably to a large extent true that these correspondents could not spare the time, and possibly the money, to come. Glenthorne is still a very difficult place to get to and times had changed. The sense of ease and well-earned leisure that Walter's friends felt after successfully winning the war had gone and, towards the end of the century, a new seriousness had developed. Most of the people whom the younger Hallidays knew were striving to a definite end, or striving to make ends meet. Even so, one remembers that Pauline Trevelyan seemed to find it easy enough to entice a brilliant company to Northumberland despite an even more formidable journey. Some people did come, and their letters are full of genuine thanks for kindness received but, in the main, it seems that high seriousness without warmth, gaiety and humour was not enough of a temptation. The place was very beautiful, but it was a long way to go to risk boredom.

In spite of the formidable nature of the owners, some people did keep up a steady correspondence, and some did faithfully visit. One who did both, in spite of a very busy life, was Benjamin Jowett. He was Regius Professor of Greek at Oxford, Master of Balliol, and the author of learned books, but his letters are less serious than Maria's. In one reply, he says: 'I quite appreciate what you say about Plato ... I am glad you like my sermon which I did not much myself. The negative part was too much for the positive part. A lady told me that some of my friends would find it an excuse for not going to Church!' One wonders if she had been helping him with remarks on Plato in the same way as she suggested subjects for Steinle. But for a kindly accident of time, Maria would certainly have been the person from Porlock who interrupted Coleridge in the writing of *Kubla Khan* in a nearby farmhouse.

One letter of Jowett's thanks Maria for introducing him to another of her long-standing friends, Lord Lytton, the author of *The Last Days of Pompeii* and very many other historical, romantic and wordy novels, all of which are on the Glenthorne library shelves. He and Maria met and corresponded regularly, both in town, and on Exmoor, for one of Lord Lytton's estates adjoined Glenthorne. Their relationship was arch, almost flirtatious, and the letters that survive are full of thanks for little gifts: pretty pencils and a paper-knife from Maria; a New Year's gift of bon-bons in a silver gilt basin and a box of teaspoons from Lord Lytton. Photographs were exchanged, and there were visits to the theatre and occasional dinners à deux – 'I suppose Mrs Grundy would have nothing to say against it?' Lord Lytton asks. There is even a copy of light verses about a donkey written by Maria and corrected by Lord Lytton, but their real link seems to have been a mutual preoccupation with the state of his health, both physical and spiritual. He sends detailed bulletins of the progress of his bronchial colds which seemed to afflict him constantly , and he apologises for not having done justice to his dinner, not because he did not like it, but because the doctor had ordered him to partake of lunch and, therefore, his appetite for dinner was impaired. Twice he apologises for unintentional bad manners when preoccupied. Obviously he suffered from the sensibility of a creative spirit. Did the middle-aged Maria perhaps see in him something of her lost lover or the romantic heroes of Jean-Paul or Goethe? Her correspondence with James Martineau, professor of mental and moral philosophy at Manchester New College, and brother of the social reformer, Harriet Martineau, was on a much higher plane. He expresses gratitude for support from those engaged in the same spiritual conflicts, and covers three sides of letter paper with small writing in answer to her enquiry on his attitude to the office of prayer. However, her correspondence with R.D. Blackmore, the author of *Lorna Doone,* is perhaps of a little more general interest. Blackmore knew the district well from visiting it with his uncle who held the living of Oare as well as that of Charles in North Devon. Blackmore was so used to having no success with his novels that when he wrote *Lorna Doone*, he did not even bother to change names of places or people. For some unexpected reason, some say because Princess

Louise had just married the Marquis of Lorne and the names were similar enough to catch the attention, this book was a success. People began to visit the district because of it, much to the annoyance of the local inhabitants, notably the Squire of Oare, Nicholas Snow. Maria took on, or was given, the job of trying to reconcile Blackmore and Snow. She did not succeed, nor did she succeed in persuading Blackmore to visit Glenthorne. In return for hampers of game, he sent a signed, illustrated copy of *Lorna Doone* and one of his exceedingly tedious novel, *Tommy Upmore*.

It was, in fact, *Lorna Doone*, rather than intrinsic beauty that first made this part of Exmoor into a tourist attraction. Walter chose it for itself alone, and now more people come for the landscape and few for *Lorna Doone* alone, but it was the fact of its being Doone country that popularised it. At first, the local people were incensed at this invasion of their privacy but now, on the whole, they thank Blackmore for providing custom for cafés and hotels, and keeping the church roof sound and the organ in repair. Many little girls in the area have been christened Lorna, and even Glenthorne can be proud of being mentioned once, anachronistically, in this seventeenth-century romance.

Maria may well have been considered a literary lion-hunter but, after all, she had one publication in her own name. In her preface to her book on Italian painters, she expressed the hope of producing similar books on the galleries of other countries. These never materialised but, while she was at Glenthorne, she undertook two pieces of research. The first resulted in: *The sculptured monuments of the fifteenth century in the Church of St Dubricius in Porlock, Somerset*, illustrated by a Torquay artist, Roscoe Gibbs, dedicated to the Earl of Devon, and published in 1882. Her interest in the monuments started, she tells us, when she first visited the church and saw a monument 'more befitting a Cathedral than a country Church.' It consisted of the alabaster effigies of a knight and his lady lying on an altar tomb surmounted by an elaborate canopy. No one seemed to know, or care, who they were and Maria set to work to find out. The book is an account of her excursions into medieval history, genealogy and heraldry, resulting in the conclusion that the figures were of Sir John Harrington and his wife, Elizabeth Courtenay. Roscoe Gibbs not only did the drawings, but wrote an explanation of them, and a description of the church, which, to many, must be the most interesting part of the book. It is a painstaking piece of work, well produced by the Torquay Directory Company, and, judging by the reviews pasted in her press copy and the number of people to whom she sent it, Maria was proud of it. There still exist letters of acknowledgement from the Secretary of the Somerset Archaeological Society, who criticised the absence of an index, from the well-known travel writer, Augustus Hare, from Henry Shorthouse, the author of *John Inglesant* and from F.D. Maurice, the theologian.

Encouraged by their success, she and Roscoe Gibbs set to work again and, two years later, another book appeared, printed again by the Torquay Directory Company, but this time for private circulation. This book is entitled *The Courtenay Mantelpiece*, the subject of which can be seen in the Bishop's Palace, Exeter. It is lavishly produced with vellum-like covers and end-papers of episcopal purple, but the matter is undeniably thin. There is, after all, a limited amount to be said about a mantelpiece, however large, ancient and beautiful, without roaming further afield for 'padding'. It comes in the class of what we now call coffee-table books, except that it is rather heavy reading.

This was the last of Maria's published books. Judging by all three publications, it seems as though the painstaking side of her nature which was willing to worry out facts correctly and minutely, had triumphed over the side which strove for an ever greater sensibility. The mood at Glenthorne had become less genial and more sober and inward-looking and one cannot help feeling that much of Walter's creation was wasted on his successors. They knew its worth, because others told them that they had something worth having but failed to relish it and rejoice in it. Halliday divided his time between his books and his public life, and Maria was occupied with her correspondence and her intellectual enquiries, while Helen, energetic, kind, prosaic and evangelical, ran the place.

Marion

There was, however, also Marion. In her youth she was rarely mentioned, except as being there, although Helen sometimes noted in her travel diary that she would have like to have explored further, but Mama and Marion would not venture. As she grew up, she was considered different and, in later life, her contemporaries referred to her as slightly deranged, while the youngest members of the family called her 'batty Aunt Marion'. It was a harsh judgement, but her relations were probably right in considering her on the whole negligible and something of a liability.

Marion, however, led an intense inner life and wrote verse with far more facility than Maria wrote prose. If her work has any value at all, which is, to say the least, doubtful, it is as an example, a horrid warning, of where the current trend of sensibility and self-examination could lead, and of how nature had been demoted from a great power to being God's agent in pointing a moral. Personal tragedy and Mrs Grundy seem to have united in depressing the Cosways' family life. The happiness and freedom that, as children, they enjoyed, changed after Sir William was killed. Elizabeth Halliday was known for independence and strength of mind: as Sir William Cosway's widow, she took refuge in religion, respectability and a very firm hold on her children. After the deaths of Eliza and Georgina, this hold tightened, no doubt as she felt she must hold on to what she had left. Halliday, as a boy, escaped to a large extent because he was sent away for his education but, as Helen and Marion grew up, their old freedom was contracted to such an extent that they were never allowed out unaccompanied for even the shortest distance, long after they must have been considered to have acquired the safe status of old maids. When they did go out it was, more often than not, to perform an act of charity. At home, reading was largely inspirational. Helen's robust constitution, physical and mental, led her to good works, but Marion sank into morbid sensibility. Marion's photograph shows her looking sprightly but, in fact, her main characteristic was gloom of the inspirational sort. She belonged to the school of thought that is reminded of death by a fine morning, because sunrise leads to sunset, and so it is with us!

One has to be careful about scoffing: she had grown up with the anxieties of prolonged illness and death, and so had quite a few of her friends, for this was the period when tuberculosis seemed always to be lying in wait for young adults. It is not surprising that there are poems on the early deaths of Eliza and Georgina (always known as Nina to her family) but what is alarming is that she is writing them in the 1860s when they had died in 1847 and 1853, and that she was still underlining their natal and fatal days.

It argues an empty life.

She has left to posterity three slim notebooks dated 1860, 1863 and 1880, but the last one is mostly her 'collected works', a copying-out of her best poems, together with favourite hymns and sermons. It is desperately serious, but taken altogether it reads very much like a parody of all the other family diarists of the time. It ends with some 'pointed scriptural truths':

> *Faith* makes a Christian.
> *Life* proves a Christian.
> *Trials* confirm a Christian.
> *Death* crowns a Christian.

All the books are a mixture of notes of impressive sermons, notes for Sunday School lessons which are not likely to have changed the lives of her pupils, although they are carefully prepared with countless biblical references, extracts from pious works such as *The Wells of Baca* by McDuff, favourite hymns and poems by herself and friends and, occasionally, such professionals as Tennyson. The tone is uniformly pious except for one startling exception, Herrick's *Gather ye Rosebuds*, and one can only think that the mention of flying time made her mistake the message. She did get the Curate of All Saints, Derby, to write in her book, but his poem is on texts from St John and starts:

> Lord Jesus, dost Thou call me
> To give my heart to Thee
> And dost Thou really offer
> Thine heart and love to me?

Nina and Helen both showed excessive piety in childhood and, from an extract in one of Marion's books, it seems that Mama was responsible for this, although she must have had apt pupils. The passage is entitled 'My dearest Mother's letter about me to Aunt Charlotte' and reads:

> My children are all well-disposed, but my sweet little Marion is my greatest comfort. Her love of holy things and the remarkable docility and gentleness of her disposition give promise of much future excellence. I wish you knew her as I am

107

sure she would interest you. She is only just six, but you cannot give her a greater pleasure than to allow her to visit the aged poor, to whom she will read a chapter in the Bible, with great feeling and propriety. My estimate of this dear child is confirmed by that of others! Her Uncle and Aunt and Lady Forbes, *all* say they never met with such a *good* child.

The saddest thing about this is that it was lovingly copied out and treasured by the middle-aged Marion. In this atmosphere, it is not surprising that one of Eliza's few literary works, written when she was ten, and faithfully copied out by Marion in 1861, should read:

Lines by Eliza Sophia Cosway to her sister Nina.

My sister, as the seasons fly
Should we not prepare to die?
For every year's revolving sun
Brings us all nearer to our home

How many, young as you and I
In their silent graves for ever lie?
And who can tell but what we both
For both may fall beneath death's stroke

Then let us to the Saviour pray
That he will wash our sins away
And pray Him by His precious blood
To make us humble, faithful, good

My sister, may the Saviour's love
Descend upon us from above
And when this life and sorrow cease
Oh, may we both depart in peace

Children of this age do often enjoy a good wallow in lugubriousness, but Eliza does seem to have had a great deal of material to work on. She was said to have been the fair, happy, lively member of the family!

It is, of course, to be expected that Marion wrote poems on her sisters. The first one to be transcribed into her last book is called

108

The Sisters. It starts:

> Nurtured in our sweet Island Home
> By fond maternal care
> The Sisters their bright course began
> A tender loving pair

and it ends:

> Farewell, loved Sisters, here we part
> On Jordan's River-side
> But, Sisters sweet, we soon shall meet
> Where Death can ne'er divide

There are 29 verses in between!

Glenthorne, however, is her main inspiration. There are lines written *Under the Ilex Tree* at evening, and *Lines on the River Lyn, written at Watersmeet*; the river's message, naturally, is 'Don't waste life; it's running away' – and yet her days must sometimes have seemed very long. There are *In Memoriam* lines written to Walter on his 'natal day' and *Glenthorne from the Sea* is on the same subject for though

> The smiling landscape spoke of God
> This lovely spot who made
> Yet *Death* hath cast his mantle down
> E'en o'er this peaceful shade.
>
> The Master dear, to rest has gone
> His sleep is deep and calm
> But that deep sleep no waking knows,
> He lies in Death's cold arm.

In her own estimation, one of her most successful works is simply entitled

> Lines on Glenthorne
>
> The Rocks that bound this Sea-girt shore
> Wild Nature's Fortress make.
> The Sea-birds build their nests afar
> But soon their young forsake.

The Dog-Rose twines her tendrils soft
With richest verdure crowned
The Fox-Glove rears her head aloft
And gladness reigns around.

True 'tis a wild romantic scene
With tender memories fraught
Of childhood's sweet but transient dream
In heart's recesses wrought.

In silent dell, in woodland shade
Which footprint scarce hath borne
Midst purple hill and mossy glade
I hail thee, dear Glenthorne.

Farewell, ye loved and cherished haunts
Where oft my steps have trod
Whose heath-clad hills with rev'rent brow
Draw up the heart to God.

The leafy boughs of Mountain Ash
Kissing the rippling wave
The Billows roll, the Ocean's foam
Intent the shore to lave.

Oh! dost not this the eye rejoice
The heart to gladness stir
And hear not we a thrilling voice
In Nature's mystic awe.

We feel it stealing o'er our souls
Deeply, yet unconfessed
A strange, mysterious, silent thrill
Lulling the heart to rest.

Farewell, sweet shades of dear Glenthorne
When far from thee I roam
Thy mossy glades, thy moonlit shades
Recall my Glenthorne Home.

She must have been entirely satisfied with this because there are no pencil corrections, as there are in some of her other poems. When, however, one has stopped laughing or shuddering at this horrible doggerel, one comes to the realisation that, however deficient her imagination and inadequate her means of expression, she was probably one of all those living at Glenthorne at that time who appreciated it most, and for what Walter would probably have considered the right reasons. It is a wild romantic scene, and it is the sense of untrodden ways which is so exciting. Moreover, it was the idea that Nature could speak directly to the spirit that was at the bottom of much of the early, pure romantic movement. It is a sad thought that, however strong the feeling, much art is needed in the expression of it, and that poetry is particularly dangerous. It is perhaps dangerous, too, for a person with this particular cast of mind to stay too long in a place like Glenthorne. The God of Church had ousted Wordsworth's God of the Hills.

The Children

Compared with Walter's day, there was a heaviness of spirit about the place, encouraged, no doubt, by a shortage of ready money. Outwardly, however, the scene looked well under control. Contemporary photographs show bearded gardeners pushing lawn-mowers round the intricacies of the rose garden, and smart tubs of plants standing sentinel round the edge of the croquet lawn. There is a charming photograph of Marion's four little nieces sitting on the grass in the nearest meadow with the breeze ruffling their hair ribbons and pinafore frills, and there are later photographs of them on their ponies, and then as young ladies on their horses. It should have been an ideal place for children to grow up and often they must have been very happy. They not only had their ponies but there were rides in the trap and picnics. Sometimes Blind Bale, the fiddler, came down to play for dancing on the lawn and, even with close supervision, it must have been possible to escape to delectable secret places.

However, in old age, the three surviving nieces, for Isobel had died in childhood, remembered oppression more clearly than pleasure. Constance, who inherited the estate, recalled how once at dinner she had dared to ask for more. 'More, Constance, more?' her father asked in such deep tones of grief and amazement that she longed to slide under the table and never dared ask again. Father, as head of the household, naturally had to keep his own strength up with a good plateful. The girls recalled that they were often hungry, though whether this was through miscalculation, meanness or a desire to inculcate self-denial, they could never decide. When they were too hungry to sleep, they would creep out of bed to huddle at the top of the back-stairs until the butler sneaked something up to them from the servants' hall. Perhaps it was bread, cheese and beer that carried them through to the great ages of eighty-eight, ninety-four and ninety-six!

Perhaps Halliday found compensation in domestic tyranny for comparative ineffectiveness outside. Still, he was away quite often which must have lightened the atmosphere and, as the girls grew up, they went on as much of a round of visits as could be managed to launch them on the marriage market. Here again, though, there was never that feeling of triumph, of having managed all things well, that Maria's parents must have had. It was rumoured that Maria's eldest daughter, another Helen, who was as strong-minded as any of her forebears, was caught just in time when trying to elope, to escape from home rather than from unruly passion. When she did marry, Halliday disliked and mistrusted her husband, although his family history was certainly as respectable as Halliday's own. The second daughter, Constance, was the 'delicate one', a character to be found in most Victorian families. Her health was considered unequal to marriage and she was not expected to live long.

The youngest sister, Lucy, was the only one to marry with her father's blessing. Halliday did his best to signify his disapproval of Helen's husband by leaving the estate to Constance, entailed on Helen's eldest son. It was assumed that Constance would live just long enough to nurse the inheritance until his grandson was old enough to take over, which she certainly did, dying when he was sixty-four! It seems also to have been assumed that the grandson would inherit no taint of alien blood.

In 1889, when she was sixty-four, Maria died of cancer. She may well have been missed by her friends, but her family seems to have missed her remarkably little. After all, there was still Aunt Helen to depend on. Although Halliday disliked his daughter Helen's husband, he did not cut off relations with her. In 1898, for some unrecorded reason, he was travelling in Canada with her. In Montreal he fell ill, pneumonia was diagnosed and in three days he was dead. Helen, had need of all her practical sense and managing ability to deal with all the formalities, arrange for his burial, provide for a suitable monument, pack up his possessions and get back to England, where Constance, who had no practical sense, and, as soon became apparent, no money, prepared to take over.

In old age, the sisters never mentioned their mother, but spoke of their father with strong, evergreen dislike, untempered by charity. Constance used to recall how, some years after she had inherited, a footman who had left her parents' service and done well elsewhere came back on a visit principally to gratify himself in telling her that Glenthorne was the meanest household he had ever encountered. It seemed as though this second generation had taken pains to prove that a life of elegant simplicity in the country was costly and to disprove the philosophical ideas, so prevalent in Walter's youth, that to live amidst the generous beauties of unspoilt nature made people, almost automatically, generous, beautiful and unspoilt.

It was just over a century since Walter's birth, but it must have seemed that everything that he had spent his life and fortune in building up must now be dispersed. His niece, Helen, however, although she was now sixty-nine and had enough money to live, with Marion, in the Cowes house, was not ready to give in. The Scottish estate had already gone, left at Walter's death to his sister Anne Johnstone's family, and disposed of to ease their money troubles. Now the Bilsington estate was disposed of. The money was used to pay bequests and legacies including Helen's and Marion's inheritance and, with their money, Helen bought two of the Glenthorne farms and managed them herself, thus emulating Katherine.

The big house was let to a succession of people, and she and Constance, with Marion, until she crossed over Jordan in 1900, lived quietly in a smaller, but very pleasant house adjoining the home farm. She managed so well that eventually they were back in Glenthorne and, twelve years after she took over, she was able to find the money to build a new school and school house in Countisbury. Thus Glenthorne went quietly on, apparently much the same as ever, but showing signs of increasing shabbiness all over the estate, until the First World War made even shabbiness respectable.

113

ENLARGING THE MIND

Lady Sybella Farquhar – 1815

Whatever their other preoccupations, all these people seemed to find the time and the money to travel and, when they did, they conscientiously kept journals. Only some of the journals have survived and, although those that have are obviously the products of literate and reasonably lively minds, taken singly they do not leave one feeling that their neglect has deprived the world of masterpieces. Taken together, however, they provide an interesting illustration of changing attitudes and conditions during the nineteenth century. Their itineraries were often similar and they visited many of the same places but often reacted to them differently. They cover only about forty years in the first half of the century but, even in that time, there is a recognisable change in ideas and attitudes. With the development of the railways, one feels as if one is watching the birth of tourism; travel becomes quicker and easier but, ironically, nationalism becomes stronger. Sybella's diary has an unmistakeably Georgian flavour, Walter is a citizen of the world but Nina and Helen are definitely Victorian English. All of them would have considered that they belonged to the Romantic school of thought and one notices that wherever they go after Glenthorne has come into being they use it as a yardstick when judging the merits of other landscapes.

We tend to tell ourselves, and each other, while being whisked through the sky to alien places, that our forebears in the last century were sensible and travelled in a more leisurely manner, but it seems from these diaries that 'leisurely' is not the right word. They certainly travelled more slowly, but only because they could not help it. When they reached their destinations, they often stayed far longer than we should contemplate but they went to them as quickly as ever they could, suffering long days of jolting in coaches over indifferent roads, putting up with poor meals and arriving with aching bodies to spend short nights in often uncomfortable and noisy inns.

Maria's parents, Sybella and Thomas Farquhar, spent three

months touring Europe in 1815. Although Napoleon's defeat at Waterloo had only just made France accessible again, they seemed constantly to be meeting friends and acquaintances on their way and, for some of the time, they were accompanied by Walter Halliday and his older brother, George.

In July, they took their own coach across the Channel on the packet and were attended by Thomas' manservant and Sybella's maid, Godfrey, who followed with the luggage in a cabriolet. Despite this, their discomforts began as soon as they reached Calais. The carriage was held up at the customs house and, as Sybella records: 'No business being transacted after seven o'clock in the evening, I was obliged to sleep without my Night Apparel.' From Calais they progressed slowly to Paris for the post-horses were heavy plodders 'taken from the plough and harnessed with ropes, which,' she writes with asperity, 'the Postillions generally stop to mend every half mile.' She had set out in search of the picturesque, so the Normandy countryside was not to her taste, being flat and, along the roads, treeless. Some of the inns were good but many others were barely tolerable and there was poverty and dirt everywhere. The worst day of all was when, on their way to Beauvais, the horses drawing the servants' cabriolet fell down and Godfrey was so frightened that they had to take her on their barouche box. With the delay caused by this accident, they were fifteen hours on the road, and Sybella was so tired that she was more than usually grateful to find a very good bed at the inn. Indeed, it had hangings so pretty that 'I was induced to take a pattern for our room in St James.' Whether the innkeeper's wife had an extra piece or whether she got Godfrey to snip off a bit where it would not be noticed is not recorded.

Having reached Paris, they stayed there for three weeks sightseeing by day and dining with friends or attending the opera or the French Theatre in the evenings. Sybella's comments are limited to what was 'very fine' or dull, but she greatly admired the Palace of St Cloud and was fascinated by all the changes that Napoleon had made. It is obvious that he had a great hold over the imagination and was already on the way to becoming a legend. Apart from this, her interests were mainly social but when they leave Paris and journey towards the mountains there is a complete change of atmosphere and one feels that this is what she had really come for. Her admiration of fine rooms and furniture had been real enough; after all, they were the background of life as she knew it but here carried to the greatest degree of grandeur; her appreciation of pictures and objets d'art was dutiful but her enthusiasm for the grander works of nature is entirely unforced.

Her transports began as they travelled from Morez to Geneva, even though the day had begun at 5 a.m. with her maid coming in looking like a ghost and announcing that she would have died in the night from violent stomach ache. She starts off:

'No language can do justice to the exquisite beauty of the country between Morez and Geneva, the ascent for some distance is very ragged, and in case of the most trifling accident happening to the Horses and Carriage, extremely dangerous and you must inevitably be dashed down precipices of hundreds of feet, there are high poles placed at the edge of the precipice to point out the road in Winter when the snow is deep on the Mountains. It is impossible to conceive the romantic scenery of the Mountains unless one has been an eyewitness to their beauties. The road winds in a serpentine manner and the Mountains richly wooded lie one beyond another till their tops are lost in the Clouds. Numberless Shepherds' huts lie scattered in the Valley and at the distance of some leagues from Geneva Mont Blanc 14,700 feet above the level of the sea and covered with eternal snows first opens on the view, and proceeding a little further, beautiful Lake Geneva situated in a luxuriant Valley and surrounded by Mountains. At Gex, as the horses were not ready, we sat under a tree to shade us from the heat of the sun and made an excellent repast on fruit, bread, and the Vin de Pays, a kind of weak Burgundy.' Here we already have those two necessities to the romantic view of things: the picturesque and the simple.

Regretfully, they paused at Geneva only long enough to work out their route for the glaciers and to cross the lake to Mme de Stael's villa at Coppet and then they went on to St Martin where they had 'a tolerable supper and good Beds' in preparation for a strenuous day ahead. Now, sightseeing in the Alps is relatively easy unless one wishes to do it the hard way but, in 1815, long before the advent of cable cars, it really was physically taxing, and quite dangerous and it is interesting that quite a few women besides Sybella were determined to see for themselves.

On Tuesday, 29 August: 'We rose at 5 o'clock and, after breakfast, mounted a Charabanc, a kind of Garden Chair drawn by two Horses, that sort of Conveyance being alone calculated for travelling in the Mountains. We passed thro' the wildest and most picturesque scenery imaginable till we arrived at Serbos, where the horses stood an hour to refresh – the situation of this little Auberge is quite beautiful. We quitted our Charabancs and went into the Salon, where the Aubergiste displayed dried flowers, the produce of the Alps, Crystals and Minerals found on Mont Blanc. I purchased several minerals. There, in compliance with the advice of the guides, we changed our intention of returning to Geneva by the same route as we had intended ... We continued our course up the Mountains, thro' Mountain Torrents and up almost perpendicular passes in the narrowest road imaginable, looking down the most beautiful tho' most terrific precipices, till the lovely valley of Chamonix spread before us. The view was, however, less fine from the rain which descended in torrents and obscured the distant prospect. The Glacier of the Bossons is the first which presents itself, a huge mass of ice extending down the mountain and forming an extraordinary contrast with the Verdant appearance of the latter. There are immense cracks or crevices in these Glaciers which are frightful to look down; they are yawning gulfs of a bluish colour, the depth of one which was fathomed was 360 fathoms – as Mr Farquhar and Mr Geffuhle preferred walking, I proceeded alone to Chamonix and, on their arrival, we dined with a party of Genevese, who had just made the excursion to Milan.'

The next day was even more strenuous. Once again, they were up at 5 a.m. though the weather was not considered settled enough to allow them to start until 9 a.m., when the two men set off on mules and 'I was carried on a chair by eight men, or rather two at a time, the rest following to relieve. After half-an-hour's march, the path was too narrow and perpendicular for the Mules, and Farquhar and Mr Geffuhle quitted them and took two long poles with a spike at the end of each, to assist them in climbing. We ascended the Path up the Mountain, which is cut zig-zag, and just wide enough for one person to pass. It requires some resolution, and a steady head, to ascend this Mountain, which is extremely dangerous. In some parts, I left the chair and walked with the assistance of the guide, carefully avoiding to look at the side of the precipices at the bottom of which the Valley of Chamonix appeared quite insignificant. After two hours, and half perpendicular ascent, we reached the top of the Montanvert, having for some time been above the clouds. It was quite cold, and I felt glad to warm myself at a fire the shepherds had kindled for the travellers. Farquhar was excessively fatigued; he had ascended as quickly as possible for two hours and a half and he, as well as the rest of the Party, were quite overcome by the exertion. From the top of the Mountain, you have the finest view of the Mer de Glace, the largest of the Glaciers. It is of immense extent between the Mountains, and it is impossible to conceive a more grand or imposing scene. We descended on the Mer de Glace and, after traversing a small part and when I could not help shuddering to see how we were surrounded by yawning, bottomless precipices of ice, and where the most trifling imprudence or accident might have precipitated us, the guides wished to persuade us to proceed across the Mer de Glace to the Jardin, a spot of ground of some extent very fertile, and entirely surrounded by Mountains of ice; as it, however, must be attended with some difficulty as well as danger, we eagerly ascended the Mountain to return to our hut to dinner. The descent as well as the ascent to the Mer de Glace is one of the most dangerous passes in the Mountain from its narrowness as well as perpendicular form. Our guides had carried up cold meat and Vin de Pays and we, as well as another Party, sat down to refresh ourselves. The Women who inhabit these Mountains can go through considerably greater fatigue than we can, as a Lady belonging to the other Party had literally walked the whole way from Chamonix, descended on to the Mer de Glace and intended to walk the whole way back. After our repast, we drew around the fire, while the guides refreshed themselves and the Shepherd produced Necklaces, Seals and Ear-rings of Rock Crystal from Mont Blanc. As the day was unfavourable, we had not a very fine view from the Mountains, though we were considerably above the Clouds. In ascending we heard several avalanches de Glace which sounded like the loudest Thunder – in the Winter and Spring, the Avalanches de Neige produce frequently the most dreadful consequences; they are occasioned by fresh snow falling on the old, or any trifling circumstance which detaches it from its original situation, when it rolls down the precipices gathering as it goes, overwhelming whatever it comes near and, at length, falling with such a violent explosion that it is felt in the valley for many leagues. From the moment we began to descend, the rain commenced and, after two hours descent, we arrived at Chamonix nearly wet thro' and tired. The descending in a Chaise à Porteurs is much more unpleasant and alarming than ascending, and I frequently quitted the chair to walk between two guides. We went to bed while our clothes were drying and, at 8 o'clock, went into the public room which was filled with English.'

It is not surprising that they took things a little more easily the next day. After once more working out the route to Milan, they went by charabanc to see the source of the Avron which Sybella found 'certainly one of the most beautiful spots nature ever formed' and goes on: 'We drove thro' a wood of tall Firs till we arrived at the Source of the River flowing out of an immense Rock of ice and dashing along with a tremendous sound. A beautiful Cascade flows down the Mountain at the top of which is the Mer de Glace, the sun sparkling against the enormous Rocks of ice and the richly luxurious Mountains which form a Panorama together with the flowers and heathers springing up on all sides conveyed the idea of enchanted ground. We sat down under a Rock and a little Paysan who had accompanied us in the charabanc from Chamonix offered to sing *The Wonders of Mont Blanc*. Other little Paysans brought milk and fruits. On our return, we encountered a most beautiful girl about fifteen, whom we stopped to speak to. I scarcely saw so perfect a face. We went to see the Pyramids of ice in the Glaciers des Bossons, returned home to dinner – a large and vulgar Party at the Table d'Hôte.'

All the ingredients of a holiday area are already there: the great natural beauty, the uncooperative weather, the souvenirs available at strategic points and the other tourists.

They made their way through the Simplon Pass where she felt 'seized with a kind of horror when the Postillion told us it was only ten days ago that a Pedlar had been murdered in the Rock and then thrown down the torrent. The savage appearance of the place was calculated for deeds of darkness and murder; the rocky sides of the mountain jutting over our heads and appearing as if on the point of falling to crush us while the Mountain Torrent, rolling in thunder from steep to steep, hurried shattered fragments of rock down its eddy, filling the dell with uproar.'

After a few days in Milan which she left 'without any regret', they proceeded to Venice to admire the art treasures there. There were fine pictures of the Flemish School, she notes, and two pictures of a Magdalen and St Cecilia by Carlo Dolci were 'exquisitely beautiful'.

Within a week they were on their way back via Padua, Vicenza and Brescia and then they went on to Turin. Everything of note is recorded, but her summing-up of Italy is damping: 'Nature has been very kind to Italy. Everything grows with much luxuriance ... and food of every description is much cheaper than in England. Nothing, however, can compensate for the want of cleanliness, and even common decency, which exists everywhere on the Continent.'

It is only when they are on their way back to Geneva, travelling from St Jean de Maurienne to Chambéry, that real enthusiasm breaks out again: 'It is impossible to find words sufficiently expressive of the beauties, magnificence, wildness, and yet great luxuriance of the Alps binding the valley ... at Aiguebelle the Alps begin to tower and, though the road from Chambéry is beautiful, yet you lose that bold description of scenery which fills the mind with wonder and admiration.' There is no doubt that nature excites her more than buildings and pictures, and that the wilder and grander the scenery, the happier she is.

They made excursions to the 'Cascade of Staubbach', Interlaken, Lauterbrunnen and Grindelwald, admiring all the time until she notes: 'As it is absurd to repeat the same words so frequently, I shall merely observe that both Farquhar and myself considered the valley of Lauterbrunnen the finest thing we had hitherto seen in Switzerland ... The Curate's house at Lauterbrunnen commands, I may almost say, the most picturesque situation in the world. It immediately faces the Cascade of Staubbach falling 900 ft. from the Rock – it stands at the foot of the Mountain, richly wooded with the Torrent dashing at the bottom and the Glaciers of Jungfrau and Brithorn to the left; I never saw so perfect a landscape.

The long tour was nearly over, and they were now on their way back to Calais via Zurich, Offenburg, Karlsruhe, Mannheim, Linz, Cologne, Brussels and Ostend. From Mannheim to Linz they sailed down the Rhine in a boat 'most habitable and commodious'. There was still much to see but only twice is her rapture aroused to anything like the pitch evoked by the scenery at Lauterbrunnen. From Zurich, they went to Schaffhausen to see the Falls of the Rhine. On the first day, they took a boat, intending to cross over to the Château of Lauffen under the Falls, but she was so terrified that they returned immediately to the shore. The next day they went by road in a calèche and viewed it from the gallery in the rock. It was all well worth it, for she says: 'I was more struck with the sublimity of this object than with anything else during the Tour ... Standing on the Gallery ... where you are covered with spray, and almost stunned with the Thunder of the Torrent, it is impossible to help being affected with the sublimity of the surrounding scene.'

Her next noteworthy experience was the journey by boat on the Rhine, not primarily because of the scenery, although this was 'a singular and beautiful assemblage of fertility and wildness', but because of 'the Barren Rocks which rise to an enormous height and on which are innumerable Castles now falling into decay. All these magnificent buildings belonged to Princes and Barons of great power in former ages and to most of them some interesting Tale is attached. Many of them go as far back as the Holy Wars. I regretted not having the time to explore some of these imposing edifices ... In no part of our Travels have I passed any Country which has conveyed the idea of the magnificence and chivalry of ancient days like that of the trajet down the Rhine.'

Among all the buildings that she did visit the only ones she regrets not exploring are monasteries or convents, generally at the top of mountains, and ancient castles, preferably in ruins, and one is reminded that, for a great many people, the Middle Ages had become the most interesting period of history. It was fifty years since serious medieval studies had begun with Bishop Hurd and Macpherson's *Fragments* and Percy's *Reliques* had appeared. Then came the imaginative response with Walpole's *The Castle of Otranto* and *Mysterious Mother* and Ann Radcliffe's *The Mysteries of Udolpho*, followed by a vast number of imitators. By 1815 there had been time for the satirists such as 'Monk' Lewis and Jane Austen as well, but still, medievalism, whether of the scholarly or Udolpho variety, held the imagination of a great variety of people. As a relief from the cult of Reason, they admired the rugged grandeur of its buildings, its simple faith, its clear-cut codes of behaviour and its mysteries, whether of the Holy Grail or of the skeleton-in-the-cupboard variety.

Picking one's way through the faded ink of the journal, with its plethora of capital letters and its lack of punctuation, one realises that the adjectives of admiration are still used advisedly and according to the prevailing rules. It is, at the least, doubtful whether Sybella had ever read Burke, Gilpin or Price, but their definitions of the sublime, beautiful and the picturesque, had by now become so much part of the language that she generally uses them correctly. Burke's *Essay on the Sublime and Beautiful*, published as long ago as 1756, provided a good deal of discussion and later in the century Gilpin and Uvedale Price had defined the half-way house, the Picturesque, so that one had a sort of scale by which to judge the natural scene. The Sublime was so far above man's own scale that it aroused feelings of fear, or even terror, while the Beautiful was smooth, calm, or even static. In between came the Picturesque where the landscape was broken, rugged, grand in places, and always various: exciting but comprehensible and, therefore, the most popular. One cannot live comfortably with the sublime; the beautiful can, by its smoothness of surface, be a little dull, but the picturesque continually feeds that important ingredient of romanticism - the imagination. To Sybella, only the Falls of the Rhine are sublime, while the moon shining on the river is beautiful. The Lake of Zug is 'very pretty, I may say beautiful' and from Zug to Zurich, at the foot of Mount Albis, it becomes 'picturesque', presumably because of its more mountainous nature which had made it necessary for a bull to be harnessed in front of the four horses, as well as an additional horse in front of the bull. Then, a few leagues before Zurich, it is once more 'beautiful'. It is, of course, at Lauterbrunnen that she finds the most picturesque situation in the world, with the cascade falling 900 feet from the rock, the mountains richly wooded and the glaciers of Jungfrau and Brithorn finishing the composition. From one point, too, there is a rainbow to be seen, 'caused by the reflection of the sun on the Cascade'. This is her idea of perfection in landscape and one with which most of us would still agree. When she calls a landscape pretty, it is almost a criticism, much as we might say 'quite nice'.

It was when they had reached Brussels on their way back, that they took time to make a journey as important as the excursion to the Alps – they visited Waterloo. Two months earlier, in Paris, they had been to the Duke of Wellington's Ball, where there were 'all the celebrated characters of the allies except the Emperors of Russia and Austria' and they had supped at the very next table to the Prince and Princess of Prussia and the Duke of Wellington, who 'had seven stars on his left breast', but they had still to see the site where the decisive battle had been fought only four months earlier.

'*Sunday 22nd* (October)' she writes; 'Rose at 7 o'clock to go to Waterloo, set off at 9 o'clock, met Ld. Ebrington on the stairs of the Hotel. The day was beautiful which in some measure compensated for the roughness of the Carriage which was more like a cart. After three hours' dreadful jolting we refreshed the horses at Waterloo and proceeded to the Belle Alliance having taken a guide who explained the position of the Armies as we went along – at the Belle Alliance we got out and proceeded on foot with the guide to Houguemont, the small House which was taken and retaken so frequently, it is in the most miserable half-burned state – We bought Buttons and Eagles picked from the dead off the field of Battle, all over the field were Mounds of new mould under which the dead bodies were thrown by hundreds. We returned by the route of Nivelles to Waterloo where the Horses were refreshing and after three hours jolting returned to the Hotel quite knocked up.' Already it was being organised as a tourist attraction and the legend was growing up, but it had nothing like the aura that it acquired later in the century. Perhaps it was still too recent and raw.

The long tour ended on Friday 27th October when, at half past four in the morning, they embarked for England from Calais, seeing the Duke of Wellington again who was on his way back to Paris. It had been a very strenuous three months and she was probably glad to be back to recollect her emotions in the comparative tranquillity of life with her young family at Polesden Lacy in its pretty, or perhaps beautiful, park and to talk about her experiences in the sociability of the season at 16 St James' Street. The Augustan age was well past and indeed it was many years since Mackenzie had made sensibility fashionable in *The Man of Feeling*, but still one felt that for Sybella and her circle, a 'well-regulated mind' was far superior to an excess of sensibility and that the restraint of the eighteenth century was still to be valued in daily living.

Restraint, however, argues that there is something to be restrained and for those who could afford the great expense and exertion of travel the picturesque landscape, and the simple life of the Alps was a valuable outlet, for it gave one an intimation of those great natural forces which, though inconvenient in daily life, enlarged and expanded the soul.

The Reverend Walter Halliday – 1844

There is a long gap of twenty-nine years before the next diary of Walter's tour in Turkey and Greece. During these intervening years, he seems to have been abroad quite often and his taking of Holy Orders and becoming Curate of Cowes was no impediment. There are books, pictures and small objects in Glenthorne which have been bought at various times in different parts of Europe, and, when in Constantinople, he keeps on referring to his last visit twenty years before. He seems to have owned the Château des Clées, his converted tower in the Jura Alps, furnished with Gibbon's library, before his marriage and, while putting his estate together, went off quite regularly, but these excursions seem to have been considered part of everyday existence. It was only in 1844 that he set off on a journey important enough to warrant a record.

This diary is very different from all the others. Obviously, this is partly because he is travelling in a different part of the world, and partly because he is the only male diarist and the wider interests and greater freedom that a man of independent means could command are reflected in it. But Walter never did quite fit into any pattern: he seemed always to be spilling over in different directions and one begins to understand his family's uneasiness about him.

His travels in Switzerland, his retreat in the Alps, his pictures and, most of all, his building of Glenthorne, all prove that he was a devoted disciple of the romantic idea of the picturesque and, reading Sir William Cosway's comments, one begins to assemble a picture of a vague, impractical character. Then, as one traces the acquisition of the estate, one has to revise this opinion: his business ideas may not have been entirely orthodox and his success may partly be owing to a good choice of agents, but he did succeed.

One has him typed as a modern romantic until one comes to his diary. He obviously delights in the natural beauty of Thrace but, just as Sybella really gets into her stride when she reaches the Alps, so Walter's record becomes ardent when he contemplates the departed glory of Greece.

An education at Eton and Oxford in the first years of the nineteenth century would not have allowed him to escape the classics, but he shows far more than a dutiful interest. It seems from Katherine's letters, written on her honeymoon, that Rome had the same effect on him. She talks of his archaeologising, reading and avoiding the many English settlers at Rome. If, however, one was beginning to think of him as an enthusiastic recluse, one has only to look at his diary to realise that it is the only one that describes people as well as places, often in thumbnail sketches of a few words that make them come alive. Ironically, although he is by far the most exuberant character, he is the only one who gives a feeling of leisure. Sybella's party spent day after day rattling along in the carriage, pausing only for rest, souvenirs or a quick look at the view and the later diaries are similar. Walter seems always to be wandering about and looking about him, whether on a boat, poking about Constantinople or wandering about Thrace. Part of this impression is probably due to the fact that he rarely had to cope with the bustle and uncertainty of inns; he generally seemed to know someone or have letters of introduction to someone in a convenient place. Originally this must have been owing to the family's careers in foreign places, for there were not only father's naval and East India Company connections but also Sir William Cosway's naval friends and Sir Walter Farquhar's army acquaintances. Walter seems to have inherited their assumption that one could be at home anywhere in the world and he seemed to acquire new friends easily.

The journal is extremely difficult to decipher. Walter's handwriting is large and flowing but he appears to have used, by way of a pen, a rag on the end of a stick dipped in jam. Capital letters, exclamation marks and underlinings abound, poetical and historical references chase after each other and the language is high-flown by our standards, although his prose style often shows a balance and exactness as well as a sonority that remind one that he was educated when oratory was important. To some of his contemporaries he had alarmingly modern ideas, but he was by now past fifty and his education owed almost as much to the eighteenth as to the nineteenth century. The little book begins with a flourish of Latin inside its marbled covers:

Perturbatur Constantinopolitani
Innumerabilis Solicitudinibus

and under that information: 'Purchased at the Bazaars of Stamboul or Byzantium 1844.' The entries, however, begin when they are leaving Malta on their way to Constantinople, so he must have copied the first few entries later. Katherine was, as usual, with him, but it is a little surprising to learn that so was his dog, Pellucino. He notes with amusement: 'The Captain's Lady asked me how I could be so long absent from my flocks and herds!!! So she evidently jumps to the conclusion that I am a Farmer – since I have a <u>Sheep Dog</u> on board. Poor Pellucino is not happy or content on board – tho' a great favourite.' One never does discover why he had his dog with him. Would he not be left behind? Or was he a gift presented by one of Walter's instant friends? Or a souvenir acquired at some earlier point on the tour? – in which case he was, one feels, likely to be one of the larger breeds such as a Maremma.

They left Malta on Monday, 29 April, and were 'All day at sea – fine bright sky – easterly wind and Sea as smooth as Glass – Chess on Board!' He goes on to describe their companions: 'The Captain a <u>Socialist</u> of the Utopian kind. Pleasant talk with Vernon, who looks very unhappy and has been, as it were, incog. with his Son this Winter – both at Rome and Naples – He tells me he was the only double Class Man of his term – which I <u>well remember</u> as we were both examined the same year of 1813 tho' he appears a much older man than myself to my seeming. He is a member and belongs to the Ashley party – and is connected with some of the highest families in Europe – His son is a fine young Man – tho' his appearance is rather against him – but I cannot agree with Madame La Capitaine that his manners are <u>mauvais ton</u> – whatever <u>her own</u> may be. Young Mr Rose is a <u>second class</u> passenger, but a <u>first rate</u> young man – he is only 24 years of age and has already been 6 years in the East and is a good linguist – he is now going to <u>Moosoot</u> (the ancient Nineveh) on the banks of the Tigris as a Merchant – He is very intelligent and has a vast fund of useful knowledge and modest withal ... Among other things he gave me a lucid and graphic account of the <u>Nestorian Christians</u> who up to very lately have maintained themselves in the Mountains near Moosoot in a state of independence, and worshipping after the primitive manner of the early Christians and are supposed to be a portion of the <u>lost</u> tribes – there are many second class passengers with whom I exchange a few words in going to see Pellucino – who lives near the Bowsprit – Amongst them is a fat English Woman married to a Turk and now returning to Constantinople after packing in the Coffee House Line at Rome. Robert our Servant finds good companions in the Grand Duke's Servants – Our vessel is clean and airy – but has not sufficient power for her length – and her Engine is faulty – but she has little motion – the Princes have the Ladies Cabin and the State Cabin off it – once mine own – the Suite are stowed

away in the Main Cabin – we have the family Cabin in the Centre of the Ship to ourselves – with four berths and the Captain and his lady are on the Poop. There are four officers and a crew of 20 men – The Commissary is a self–appointed Nigaud – I do not think them friendly to Louis Phillipe but they are not <u>Jacobins</u> – they consider his <u>death</u> will be the commencement of the <u>End</u>.'
And so, in a few pages, we have it all vividly in front of us, together with political and historical asides: the grand passengers, the disappointed man with the plain son, the clever, hopeful young man, the snobbish lady, the fat lady; all collected in one slow boat under the Captaincy of a 'Utopian Socialist', and the observation of a restless, lively young man of fifty-two!

They sailed gently on, rounding Cape Matapan and passing through the Ionian Islands which roused many reflections on Greece past and present. It was a fine moonlit night and, by 6 a.m., they anchored in the Sira roadstead. Sira, he noted, was a pretty white town on a hill, with a good harbour, but as squally rain had begun, he did not go ashore but contented himself with watching the coming and going of other people. The Vernons left them for Athens but, in exchange, there came on board numbers of Turks, 'among others a Bey of noble mien bringing treasures to the Porte from Mehemet Ali. The Turkish Ambassador to Spain came on board to visit the Princes. Prince Galitzin, a Russian, came as a passenger to Egypt, a misshapen, deformed man.' Once again he manages to convey his inextinguishable interest in bustle, colour, and strangeness, even if, as here, nothing comes of it for it was, he notes, 'a squally night with showers and a heavy swell' and adds, with the smugness of a good sailor, 'few remained out the dinner.' Towards morning, when they entered the canal of Scio and sailed into the Bay of Smyrna, they reached smoother water. The entry for 2 May starts with 'Smyrna at sunrise.' Here he did land, and went with Ross to visit another friend before making a complete circuit of the bazaars, and seeing his first camels. It was not, it seems, his first visit, because he writes: 'Recognise the green hills and ford by which I approached the Town in former times – the Inn, as before, close to the water.' They left Smyrna at 5 p.m., saw Lesbos at midnight by full moon and passed the Troad in the morning. Going through the Dardanelles reminds him that here Darius first crossed into Europe and Alexander into Asia, and then, at last, on Saturday, 4 May, they reached their destination: 'We rounded the Golden

Horn – and the facing enchantment of Constantinople was before us!!!'

To Walter, history, legend and the present, are inextricably entangled and interdependent, so we can appreciate his pleasure when he writes: 'I observed with delight in the Hellespont a great flock of Pelicans. Just in the wedge of <u>Battle Array</u> as described by Old Homer and innumerable flocks of wild geese, cranes, etc. which existed in his time also, and may account for his adopting themselves, and their habits, so often in his beautiful similes.'

They settled in at an hotel here, the Hotel d'Angleterre, and then set off immediately with a guide for a preliminary tour, starting at the garden of the former British Palace, then going through the High Street of Pera to the 'Frank and American cemeteries where there is a beautiful view of Scutari and the Golden Horn with a part of the Bosphorus.' They saw the tomb of 'Lieut. Malcolm who died of plague in 1837', then came back by the Turkish Cemetery at Pera to dine at the Table d'Hôte and make the acquaintance of their fellow guests.

This was the beginning of a programme of exhaustive and, no doubt, exhausting sightseeing, and they walked, rode and went by caique, to see all that they could, finding time to re-visit places of especial interest or atmosphere. They toured the bazaars, buying as souvenirs the book in which the journal was kept, a camel bell and an 1825 edition of the *Thousand and One Nights* in French, which Walter inscribed and presented to Katherine. They visited the Greek and Jewish quarters, noting their different atmospheres, and the graveyards which Walter says, 'are very interesting places, the fine dark Cyprus contrasting well with the white-turbaned Moslem Tombs with their Green and Gold ornamental writing and indicating the Repose of the Grave.'

Walter was invited by the Grand Duke (he never tells which Grand Duke) to go with him and his suite to the Seraglio and Mosques. He passes through the Outer Court 'which is open to all the world and there are some fine decaying Old Trees inhabited by the Stork' and then he went through the gardens with the Pope's Doctor to the Water Gate of the Harem, and found the Grand Duke just landed from the Barracks. But, although the company was grand and varied enough and the gardens worth seeing, all beautifully laid out in the European way, still, it was disappointing for 'the crowd was too great and all done in a hurry.' Later that day, they watched three to four thousand soldiers parading in the great square, but this, too, was disappointing for, he says, 'In adopting the European Dress, the Turkish Soldier has ceased to be <u>Asiatic</u> – but he has by no means become <u>European</u>, and a more wretched race of striplings never existed.'

The next day he visited 'Another very curious object', the Jews' graveyard, 'so densely strewn with headstones that it brought to my remembrance the Vision of Dry Bones in the Valley – by the prophet Ezekiel.' He describes places and buildings painstakingly, but there is all the time a note of sadness at decline, and a certain amount of disapproval which come through all his energetic description. He had been there about twenty years before and, on his first day's entry, we get a hint that things are not what they used to be: 'Our Guide takes us to the Garden of the former British Palace, now a heap of ruins – I recognise the terrace where in days of yore I walked with Hamilton after dining at the Palace.'

He devotes pages to describing exactly how the murder of the Janissaries was carried out, how in 'the course of three days 10,000 of these unfortunates were slain in cold blood', so that the Sultan could have exclusive power for his Europeanising reforms. Walter is horrified, obviously, at the treachery, but is also doubtful about the wisdom of the reforms. The previous week he had visited Scutari and 'traversed the great plain where the Soldiers assemble previous to an Asiatic campaign. 'Scutari,' he records, 'is a large place, but its Grave Yards are peopled thick as the leaves of Vallombrosa in Autumn – vast alleys of the Mournful Cypress.' In view of the events of the next decade, this sounds prophetic. Disapproval takes over next, for he writes: 'It was here where we passed much time waiting for the Howling Dervishes – a very painful and degrading exhibition!' Presumably, he felt there was room for reform here.

The excursion finishes when 'Ross, K. and I reposed in a Turkish Coffee House under the shadow of some trees – How altered is the State of Turkey – We could not have done this in my former visit.' This sounds like disapproval or, at least, regret again, although Katherine might well have been grateful for the relaxation. The experience did not deter them from visiting the Dancing Dervishes next day and that he found a 'far more curious and unobjectionable exhibition than that of yesterday.'

All in all, it sounds as if the visit to Constantinople had been a depressing and disappointing experience after his high hopes on first seeing the Golden Horn. One is tempted to wonder if he was a little older than he thought, but his feelings become a good deal clearer in a long elegiac summing-up as they left to sail up the Bosphorus: 'Adieu to Constantinople ... Nothing can exceed the lovely shore of this strait, where Europe and Asia almost touch hands, a land rich in classical lore – and full of touching episodes from the period of its first conquest until its final overthrow under the Constantines – The Poetry of its ruined Walls – What can be more poetic than their wild flower aspect? All now sweetly harmonised by the Nightingale and Stock Dove – who can look on them but with respect and admiration when they remember that they have sustained upwards of 20 sieges and rarely succumbed? Who can think on this splendid city of Many Masters and not regret her declension even under Mussulman sway – It was a neutral ground for Europe and it will assuredly become a battle field of Blood. The Turk must depart but will the Successor of the Turk be less Barbaric? The Evil Genius of the Mussulman is his Religion – the Turks themselves are generally kind, humane, honest, liberal, hospitable, above all truthful. What is the Greek – What is the Russian? Sultan Mahommed by his Reforms and his annihilation of the Janissaries has hastened the decline of the Ottoman. Stamboul is no longer what I remember it – the haughty spirit of the Moslem is confounded and humbled – without – within – around – all is decay, her very reforms are merely so many acknowledgements of her incapacity for Self Government and nothing remains of the beauteous Queen of the Bosphorus but her unrivalled Horn of Gold and the lucid Perami which washes her feet. I for one admire the interior of Constantinople – where you still may meet all Nations with all Manners – and all costumes jostling each other in her scented Bazaars – her long narrow lanes and sloping declivities: there is something unlike all else here, and the wooden Houses with their Brown Roofs relieved against the Blue Sky and set in Emerald Green of surpassing richness in colour which is everywhile sobered down by the mighty gloom of the Chaste Cypress – One of the wonders of Constantinople is that with such a population – (with the exception of the Bazaars) the Town appears silent and sad and deserted in accordance with Turkish Gravity – the finest race of men here are the Turkish Boatmen – Galata is a busy thriving suburb founded by the Genoese and you may still trace its walls – and from its Tower is a magnificent view – Pera stands partly on three Hills and is also a thriving place – The Storks have very much diminished and even the nations of Dogs have dwindled away with the passing dynasty of their Masters.'

Walter is obviously practising his eloquence while making a suitable summing-up of his impressions but he is also summing up himself and his interests. There is all his energy and his propensity for noticing things and people and generating excitement. In the middle of his criticism his appreciation of landscape comes through, his noticing of colour and form that is far more exact than a mere recording of the picturesque or the beautiful. By our standards he certainly indulges himself in fine writing but his observation is not vague, nor are his classical and historical allusions. All this, however, is overlaid by the uneasy political situation. The ever-present worry about the balance of power between East and West was particularly strong at this time, and the Europeanising of Turkey was not only death to romanticism but a symptom of unrest and disintegration. It is not surprising that the antiquarian and nature lover got swamped by the politically minded man of the world. Looked at from the angle of Uvedale Price, the landscape was fine, but the figures were all wrong and the ruins far too recent.

The next part of their travels was altogether more lighthearted. They stayed at Therassia, 'a sweet Bay backed by green and wooded hills and intersected by lanes full of flowers and Birds as well as walks on the Sea Shore', and explored the countryside from there. They went by caique, 'four oars and a Steersman', to the Black Sea admiring the villages, the porpoises and the fishing stations and remembering the voyage of the Argonaut before they landed and spent two hours on shore in 'the ancient land of Thrace'. They returned to Therassia after a most delightful excursion and went for a walk up the Valley of Nightingales. It was idyllic but Walter remembered that 'Therassia was the place where Medea scattered some of her poison in pursuit of Jason.'

The next day, Wednesday, 22 May, after 'exploring before breakfast' they rode 'to Belgrade and the Bends through the Valley of Nightingales then across a hilly green pass to the aqueducts of Justinian.' They noted Lady Mary Wortley's house before going on to the Bends, 'which are large Reservoirs of Water or Lakes dammed up artificially in the most sequestered lawns or

Savannahs in the Forest – Constantinople is supplied from hence and the <u>Forest</u> is <u>sacred</u> lest the <u>axe should divert the stream</u>.' They rode back past the embassies of England, Austria, Russian and Prussia. It was a long and varied day but what interested Walter most was the scenery: 'The whole of this day's scenery,' he notes, 'reminded me very much of Yarner Mills, Porlock, Horner, Cloutsham, Brendon, Badgery, Oare, Spoonaway, Markaway, etc. Thrace is the North Devon of the Bosphorus and the Black Sea!!'

Even in this idyllic country they did not manage to avoid military trouble which, in some form or other, seems to occur in almost all nineteenth century travel accounts. Thursday, 23 May began well when they went to the heights 'opposite those where we rambled last evening – above the Sultan's Palace.' There they found 'exquisite scenery – the air alive with sounds and smells and bees and birds and all kinds save the cuckoo.' He goes on, 'We crossed into Asia in the Sultan's Valley so celebrated for its treaty where the Russians and Turks shook hands like Olympus and Homus (?) do at this bight of the Bosphorus. The valley full of large ornamental Plane Trees and its green bosom studded with Cavalry and Tents of the Prophets. Take horse for the Giant's Mountain riding thro' a country wonderfully like my own in <u>all</u> its features – Cheriton, Bridge Ball and so forth. A fine view from the Giant – but his grave all a Hum.' It was on the way back through the camp that they had looked down on, that they met trouble: 'On returning through the Camp, fracas with the Soldiers – obliged to ford a deep wet marsh – still foiled and Menaced by a swarthy Egyptian and his Damascus Blade.' There was disappointment on the next day too, for although he walked for three hours over the Thracian Hills and sequestered lanes, so like home, and carved his name on a beech tree he never heard the cuckoo, although 'it <u>used</u> to sing in Thrace.'

After five days in Thrace, they set sail again, noticing where Lord Byron swam as they passed through the Dardanelles, and soon reached Smyrna. They spent only one day here, but Walter went off to do some sightseeing and here his theological training apparently saved him at one point from being taken in when he was shown the ruins of an old church. 'Many strangers,' he remarks, 'imagine they look upon the ruins of one of the seven Churches. But when St Paul wrote, and St John, the visible Church was merely an <u>assemblage</u> of Christians – the Iron hand of Persecution even rendered their assemblies secret and fluctuating from place to place. It was not until the third, or even fourth, Century that the first Churches were built – and St John in the Revelations is writing to the Churches of Smyrna, Sardis, Ephesus, Laodicea etc. in this primary sense – tho' doubtless Churches may have been afterwards built to consecrate the recollections and traditions of the earlier, primitive Times.' He is more than ready to be impressed legitimately but not to be taken in!

The next day brought them in sight of Greece and, as at Constantinople, enthusiasm breaks out: 'At length rounding Cape Sunion descried the immortal Temple of Minerva on the Summit. 9 Columns in front are yet perfect and three lateral ones – Agenis and Salamis soon were recognised and in the Background the Cloud Capt Acropolis, Lycabettos, the Musoa – columns of Jupiter Olympus close to the banks of the Ilissus – flanked by the grey yet ever classic and beauteous Hymettus – the horizon closed in by Pentelicus. The Vale of Attica looked green and smiling as of yore as we passed the Old Port of Piraeus and shot round into almost as perfect a harbour as the world can boast – narrow jaws – deep swallow – and land locked.' One finds oneself hoping very much that Greece will not disappoint.

Before the excursions began, however, eight days quarantine were to be endured. Walter is optimistic about this; it seems that, so long as there are other people to talk to and, if possible, something to look at, he is prepared to be content. He remarks, 'The Harbour full and a gay scene which is of some importance a we are to look upon it for the next eight or ten days – Adieu to the Iberia and her Captain and our fellow Passengers – landed at our Prison House – the parded Rothwell taking command of the party – the usual cries, quarrels, explanations, shrugging and all other manner of Dumb Show and then the Spoglio and Bath and to Bed.' The next day, he reports: 'Still in Spoglio – at Breakfast the Curtain rises and there appear four French Cooks with their White Waistcoats and Night Caps in the most approved fashion – Robert (their servant) with his Sash round his Waist looks like a rope dancer. A gale from the South West tempers a hot sun ... K. and I find our fellow prisoners agreeable – Pollen a gentleman, Hawkins an Architect. Long talk with the Greek who fears to be swallowed up by the Russian Bear.' It is a graphic description, but Katherine must have felt it lacked essential information for, pinned into the diary at this point is a small paper covered in her clear writing: 'The Party who were landed on the Lazaretto at Piraeus (as coming from Constantinople),' she informs us, 'and compelled to eight days Quarantine were <u>our two selves and manservant and Dog</u>, Rothwell, an English Merchant, who likewise possessed Property in *Greece*, which caused him to make the long Trajet once a year to collect his Rents ... and two young English Artists – perfect Gentlemen – with Cultivated Minds – sent out to <u>Asia Minor</u> to make Sketches of the Remains of Noted Buildings (for British Museum) of which their Portfolios were full – and they were very kind in allowing us a sight of all – <u>Pollen</u> and <u>Hawkins</u> and we had much pleasant talk with both ... Rothwell, the eldest of the Party and a Man of the World, took upon himself to manage <u>everything</u> for us connected with Quarantine living – and regulations – and he fed us well – and we Squared Accounts with him, when we quitted our Prison, and we all went on to Athens together – and remained some time together at our Hotel there immediately under <u>the beautiful Acropolis</u> which looked so lovely by moonlight. "Spoglio" means that we all had to give up our entire wardrobe, Books – Papers – everything for 24 hrs. fumigation. We had each to be cleansed in a Warm Bath – then clad in the Garments prepared for us – Curious Figures we were. We took our exercise on the Beach of Quarantine Buildings – whence we could see the fine Port and <u>Shipping</u> of all Nations – a Newcastle Collier among them – And we looked over the pretty Hills and Country enclosing the Harbour.' It is only in contrast with Katherine's measured information that we realise how racy and impressionistic Walter's journalising is. Katherine's description of Pollen and Hawkins and Rothwell leaves us feeling well informed but when, a little later on, Walter reverts to them and describes them more fully, they are alive and present with us: 'P. a most amiable fellow Etonian – with the finest and most childlike feelings of his young days – speaks like Washington Irving writes – he has made a most interesting tour – but the soil was prepared to imbibe the refreshing shower – a fellow of Merton and a good fellow too – Hawkins clever – but more crude and more confident – R. an amusing audacity with his stories – crediting us for a long swallow – an obliging man however to whom we are much indebted.'

In a situation where laziness, or at least inactivity, could well be assumed, Walter seems to be endlessly active and energetic. He has long talks with their Greek companion about the present state

134

of Greece, he walks endlessly as far as he is allowed and examines the shipping daily, recording the nationality and destination of each vessel and, if possible, who of interest is aboard. He describes the harbour of Piraeus in terms of England: 'The West Side of the incomparable harbour of the Piraeus resembles Bossington with the distant hills of Dunkery, the Eastern side reminds me of Aldbro' and Orford Sands and Windmills.' And then in more practical terms: 'It is a most perfect harbour with a narrow neck and large deep basin within – in the North East Corner is the bight where the Quarantine is – the harbour then deepens to the northward where there is a fair sprinkling of houses.' When he is not walking and talking or going out in the quarantine boat, he is journalising or reading Thompson, while Pollen and Hawkins sketch. No wonder, when it is time to leave, he is able to say, 'Adieu to Quarantine where we have not fared ill.'

Athens could well have been a disappointment, for he is obviously as worried about modern Greece as about Turkey. On his way from Malta to Constantinople he records: 'Come in sight of Cape Matapan and enter the Archipelago – passing close to Cerigo – now the Botany Bay of the Ionian Islands – once the favoured abode of Venus!! ... What a Country is Greece! She has regained her liberty and been a kingdom of some Years' Date – and still she looks forlorn and depopulated and as hungry as in the worst times of the Ottoman Despoliation! I swept the shore of Sparta with the Glass – but all was desolate save one small Town basking in the Sunshine – No flocks, no herds, no shepherds, no living soul – nothing save the Wild Bird hovering over the sharp, cold grey ridges of Slate Stone!' The barren and forlorn state of the landscape worries him again as he looks about him from the lazaretto. 'Our Port,' he observes, 'is surrounded by some graceful Hills but hard and barren – Ancient Greece never could have supported its numerous population in such a country. Ages of neglect and misrule must have washed the soil from the surface – As my Greek friend observes – even the rivers have departed and are lost – you may find the Conduits and Aqueducts.' The present Royal Family did not inspire him with confidence either, nor did he take to their subjects when, one Sunday evening, he 'saw the King and Queen dining on a sort of Esplanade, when the Athenians were assembled for Sunday pastime – she is a fair, ruddy person without expression and his is a hard, vulgar countenance – expressive of some determination – It is impossible to picture a more motley assemblage than the existing spectators – bad taste, bad dress – bad manners, "America in the East". However, these are early times.'

Depressing as this is, it yet has no effect on his worship of 'The Glory that was Greece' which is, as it were, embalmed in his mind. Just as Sybella's diary takes on a new note when she reaches the Alps, so Walter's record takes on new excitement when he explores Athens. Sybella naturally uses the language of the Picturesque school, while Walter tends to sound like a translation of Homer.

As soon as breakfast was over on their first day in Athens, they went 'to procure money' and to pay a social call on Sir Edward and Lady Lyons (who were out) and then he starts as he says: 'to coax Kit up the Acropolis.' Kit, older and stouter than Walter, no doubt did find the climb tiring but, as soon as they were really on their way, he probably would not have noticed even if she had quietly dropped dead, he is in the grip of such enthusiasm. They climb up, 'passing the Temple of the Winds – an Octagonal Building – with the eight winged winds of Heaven – and beauteous – see at a short distance the Gate of the Agora – ascend the time worn steps of the Acropolis – the Cave of Pan – the prison of Socrates – the Pnyx – Areopagus – all open now to the view – but what pen can describe the treasures of the Sacred Mount of Ancient Greece!! Not mine.' This does not deter him from trying! He goes on: 'A New Temple of Victory (supposed to have been erected after the battle of Salamis) is a very beauteous thing of the Ionic Order – then you wander thro' the Propylaeum choked up with shafts – and Frieze and Architrave and Moulding and Bas Reliefs – which add so much to the effect – the wondrous Parthenon yellow and wrinkled with age – and mutilated by the changes and chances of so many ages still a Chaste and Severe Virgin. The Eye wanders from its Southern Façade over the most lovely of all landscapes – Aegina, The Morea, Cithoerea – The Vale of Olives, Pontilicus, Hymettus and the gigantic remains of the Temple of Jupiter Olympus near which wanders the brook Ilussis – You then gaze with delight at the Temple of Erechtheus and Minerva Polias, which is the most interesting from its fabulous and architectural celebrity. Thus hour upon hour flies away and tho' the objects are few and distinct and each one of an intrinsic merit – the eye passes from one to the other anxious but unable to grapple with any one – This is the <u>work of time</u> and the eye of Science must correct and restrain the <u>wanderings of Enthusiasm</u>.' This last observation could well be considered as holding the key to Walter's character. Enthusiasm is always there in abundance but the eye of Science is constantly on the watch to restrain excess and in this he shows that, in spite of some advanced ideas, he is still rooted in the eighteenth century.

Nothing in the rest of the journey quite came up to this morning of intense excitement exploring all that was to be seen, but one morning he set off at 6 a.m. with a guide to climb to the top of Hymettus. He got there, in spite of the difficulties caused by the 'shillity hill' and the occasional disappearance of the road, in two and a quarter hours and was well rewarded by the wild flowers at his feet and the glorious wide views. 'A few Goats and wild looking horses were,' he wrote, 'the only living objects – and it was a solemn place to ramble which I did for more than an hour and then descended to the Convent where after a moderate lunch and drinking at the source of the Ilusis I returned to Athens laden with a fine olive stick and some stones as a Memorial of my visit.' In the afternoon he set off again, taking his servant, Robert, as his companion, to the Parthenon where they examined the figure of Victory taking off her sandal, and then they went into the cave of Pan, in spite of its steepness and the fact that Pollen had had a bad fall there that very day. They returned by the Temple of Theseus and he ended the day by dining at Sir Edward Lyons' house in company, he thought, with all the other English in Athens.

Very often, the eye of Science was at work before enthusiasm could take over. He is doubtful about 'the <u>said</u> site of Academe which is very problematical' and, visiting the Areopagus where Paul and Socrates preached and being shown Socrates' 'prison House of Death and Hemlock', he remarks: 'It requires the <u>Enthusiasm of Faith</u> to credit the <u>Extravagance of Tradition</u>.' He is not a particularly gullible tourist but still he never seems to allow these extravagances to get in the way and upset his good humour or spoil his enjoyment. After his strictures on the Royal family and the citizenry he concludes that day's entry with: 'As the sun declines behind Parmis (?) it became delicious – What a picture is Athens? and set in such a frame' and, after the slight disappointment of finding a friend's grave marked with 'A rather affected piece of Latinity,' he went on to the Stadium and the

Bridge of Hadrian 'under the eastern side in face of Grey Hymettus – and amid the deepest and most poetic solitude' he gazed 'on the inimitable framework of this land of Fable!!!'

It is interesting that, although Walter was such a keen disciple of the new architecture and the picturesque and obviously had no desire to build a Palladian house and classical temples in North Devon, he still worships ancient Greece as much as the previous generation did. He says of Athens that it wants the three requirements of the English landscape: wood, water and verdure, 'and so', he adds, 'does Edinburgh, yet,' he insists, 'both Capitals are in their way astonishing and perfect.'

As a disciple of Uvedale Price he acknowledges that one must fit one's building to one's landscape and that England and Athens are very different, but it is Athens that inspires worship for what it is and what it represents. There is, after all, no reason why one should not have the mental agility to admire the Parthenon as well as an Alp and a blasted oak but still one is not quite prepared for the sacred quality of the enthusiasm accorded to the whole landscape of Greece. One cannot help wondering if it grew from a feeling of natural affinity or from the conditioning of a Public School and University education. If he had not been to Eton and Oxford, would he have felt less for Athens? It would have been interesting if Walter had left a journal of his Alpine tour or if Sybella had visited Greece and recorded her travels!

The diary leaves us in mid–air or rather in mid-Athens. There must have been at least one more volume; as it is, we have no idea how long they stayed or where they went next or if anything else was as exciting as the Acropolis, but before the winter set in they had returned with their mementos to add to their collection at home in the Thrace of South West England.

Maria Farquhar – 1846–1852

Walter's diary was written to be kept and re–read, if only by himself and Katherine, and to make sure that it was reasonably legible and understandable Katherine had gone through it, annotating here and there. Maria Farquhar's diary, though started like all the others as she set out on a journey, was kept up for six years and consisted of hasty scrawls – reminders, and sometimes safety valves for herself alone. It starts two years after

Walter's stopped, when Maria was twenty, but compared with Walter's, it is so sedate that one might have thought that he was twenty and she fifty–two. This was, no doubt, partly because she was travelling with Mama, and Sybella was certainly not the person she had been when she had started her diary thirty-one years earlier.

Except for her own diminished energy and the existence here and there of stretches of railway, Sybella cannot have found travelling conditions between London and Paris very different. Although the war was now long over they were not greatly improved. They crossed from Folkestone to Boulogne on the *Prince Ernest* steamer and were lucky to arrive in only two and a half hours because, according to Maria, 'The weather was bad, the sea rough and the wind against us.' They stayed the next day, 18 October, at Boulogne, going to church in the morning as it was Sunday, and then visiting the cathedral in the afternoon.

After only a day in Paris they went on to Fontainebleau, but the spring of the carriage broke. Maria was able to fill in time visiting the room where Napoleon had signed his abdication and read a copy of his actual letter but, no doubt feeling soured by events, she remarked that the room was 'in the French gilt style, rather low' and that the garden was stiff and formal. The next morning she was able to go all over the garden at Fontainebleau as it was a fine day, but the delay caused by the broken spring meant that they were late in leaving and were 'nearly upset in the dark near Lens by Postboy leaving the horses' and, when they did arrive, they found the Hôtel de l'Ecu very bad and dirty.

After a wet and miserable journey they reached Lyons by the end of October and were soon on their way through Provence, travelling every day until they reached Nice on 8 November. Even though they were delayed by yet another mishap at Bagnolles when the box broke, Maria seems to have enjoyed this part of the journey. She noted Roman remains, bought nougat at Montélimar and plums at Bagnolles and enjoyed the prettiness of the vine, olive and orange growing country. The views were beautiful, the weather at last fine and hot and Nice itself she thought exquisite. The Riviera was definitely her sort of country. Two days took them round the corniche to Genoa, admiring the churches, the views, and the palms waving in the breeze as they went and, when they reached Genoa, they found the Hotel de Londres very good. There followed an uncomfortable journey by sea and by coach to Rome, where, after a few days in the Hotel Meloni, they moved into their own home and began to order their lives until they felt truly at home.

A routine was soon established. Generally this consisted of reading and writing in the morning, sightseeing combined with exercise in the afternoon and sociability in the evening. There was hardly a garden, ruin, house, picture gallery or view that could be reached on foot, horse or donkey or in a carriage, that was not visited, but Maria is only occasionally stirred to note more than the barest facts. A typical entry reads: '16th May. Went to Villa Patrizio in the afternoon, lovely day, very warm, Mrs Sartoris in evening.'

It is very disappointing, but an occasional amplification gives some idea of what she really appreciated. On her way to Naples on an extended sightseeing tour, she stayed at Albano which she thought a beautiful place with exquisite scenery. One evening she went for a walk and afterwards wrote: 'Walked towards Marino, beautiful scene of moon upon Castel Gandolfo, peasants, goats and Capucin friar ascending the hill, a cross and the distant Campagna.' She dutifully records ruins and their dates but, when she went to Pompeii, her entry reads only: 'Beautiful day, left Castellamare for Pompeii, three hours seeing it, saw a little garden quite recent, returned to Naples having dined at the Hotel.' It does not seem to have been as inspiring as the moonlit walk at Albano and it is not clear whether the mention of the three hours implies thoroughness or boredom.

After a stay of eighteen months, they prepared to return to England by a different route. Any misgivings that they might have felt were justified. On 2 May they embarked at Civita Vecchia in *The Pacha* bound for Gibraltar. By the 5th they were in open sea and, although the weather was fine, it was 'all rather uncomfortable' and, by the 8th, it was a less fine day with 'much wind and more motion' and they spent 'a horrible night of pitching outside the port.' They landed the next day in torrents of rain, but all was well for 'Capn. Grey came to see us, everything so neat. English soldiers so orderly, drank tea at the Greys'.' Gibraltar, in fact, proved to be home from home, with plenty of friends and relations and the added interest of new scenery and the monkeys. When they left for Lisbon it was with Captain Grey in the steamboat *Tiger* and the journey was, for once, uneventful. In Lisbon sightseeing began immediately: views were pretty but buildings, on the whole, less so and Maria saw her first, and presumably last, bull fight, which she pronounced 'not cruel but unpleasant to look at.' By 13 June 1848 they were back in Southampton, having felt 'great delight' on first seeing the coast of Devonshire. When, on the next day, they got back to London, Maria thought the 'look of business wonderful.'

In June 1850 they set out again but this time for a health cure at the spa of Homburg in Germany. Once there they soon settled into a routine that must have been more suited to Sybella than to her daughter, drinking the waters, sitting in the gardens while listening to the band, taking tea with the other invalids and occasionally going on short excursions to places within easy reach such as Königstein and Frankenstein. In place of the balls and dinners of Rome they tended to have supper in their rooms and go to bed early.

However, they did go to one concert which produced the most memorable experience for Maria. For the first time she heard a piece called *Traumbilden* by a composer called Lumbye. It was played by a violinist called Thomas and she enjoyed it so much that she noted in her diary whenever she heard it and asked for it to be played whenever there was an opportunity. Although she heard it as a violin solo, it must originally have been a song because the lyric is written out at the back of her diary. It is a sentimental little ballad about a young girl falling asleep in the sun and dreaming. It is not great poetry and presumably the music was not great either but it comes as something of a relief that Maria could be merely sentimental.

The cure was deemed to be completed at the end of August and they set off back to England, staying a few days in Frankfurt first so that Maria could have a good look at the picture gallery. The return journey went much more smoothly and the only contretemps mentioned was having to climb a hundred stairs to their rooms at the Hôtel de L'Europe in Brussels. They stayed in Brussels for a while and, first of all, made a pilgrimage to Waterloo.

In the thirty-five years since Sybella had seen it, only a few weeks after the battle, it had been well organised for the tourist trade. They were taken to La Belle Alliance by carriage and then the carriage returned while they were taken in hand by a guide and conducted over the field but, she writes indignantly, 'mound of Belgian Lion frightful, spoils look of field.' Many people objected to the Belgian memorial, feeling that, in view of their performance at the battle, it showed lack of taste, but Maria seems to have been shocked by its lack of aesthetic taste quite as much as by its moral obtuseness and her mind is still on aesthetics when she notes that the view from the top is fine; then she recalls herself and goes on: 'Saw where Blücher advanced with Prussians, the farm of La Haye Sainte gallantly withstood by German legion – marks of bullets still there, passed St Jean on way to Waterloo when saw on our return the chapel where dead were put and which was a hospital at time of battle for wounded, went to see mound of Earth over which three Scotch pines were planted and 400 private soldiers buried, the simplicity of their grave touching and appeals more to our taste than the spot where Lord Anglesey's leg is buried – thick forest covered the country at the time of battle, now cut down – day was very cold and windy but fine. Château of Houguemont to the left on returning. 54,000 Duke had. Nap. 75,000.' One wonders what Sybella's sentiments were on revisiting it. Maria's most lasting memory was of the Belgian monument!

After this she was free to look at buildings and pictures. She visited the sculptor, Grefs, and then went on to admire the stained glass and the monuments in the Cathedral of St Gudule and the Gothic tower of the Hôtel de Ville. She would obviously have enjoyed spending a long time in Brussels but, a fortnight after their arrival, bad news about the health of her sister, Barberina Milbanks, hurried them back to England and they arrived just a month before she died.

In spite of the rigours of the journey, Sybella must have felt that the waters of Homburg did her good for by August of the next year they set off again. But less time was spent in taking the waters and by the end of September they had settled in Frankfurt for a month, which obviously suited Maria better. She enjoyed visiting the Jews' Quarter, which she thought very picturesque, and the curious historical buildings but, above all, she was able to go at leisure to the picture gallery and indulge what had now become her greatest interest. Even before she had the good fortune to meet Steinle in the gallery and, through him, Leighton, the entries had grown much longer with details of the pictures she had seen. She had two friends, Mrs Orme and Lady Caroline Forbes, to drive and drink tea with, and there were occasional little evening concerts. Even though she was an indefatigable walker and a dutiful admirer of views, it was the cultured, urbane life that roused her enthusiasm. Her mother at the same age was most deeply stirred by mountains and torrents but, to Maria, the picturesque was a matter of old buildings rather than wild landscapes, and her strongest feelings were roused by music and by pictures, preferably of people in the grip of emotion. Her mother's generation had made a great effort to get back to nature and to immediate experience: it must surely have seemed to them that Maria and her contemporaries were already in retreat.

Maria was, no doubt, happy that after leaving Frankfurt, they were to settle for a while in Paris. Their first stop was at Düsseldorf, where she just had time, by getting up early, to visit the cathedral where Steinle's angels adorned the ceiling of the choir, and to see some pictures by Meister Wilhelm, Van Eyck and Memling before they left for Brussels. Here she had two days to look at as many pictures as possible, before they caught the Grande Vitesse and, in nine and a half hours, they were in Paris. Lady Farquhar's old friend and travelling companion of 1815, Mr Geffuhle, came to visit them but Maria's most constant companion was Miss Louisa Mackenzie. Together they visited the Louvre, read Faust and went to concerts with other members of the cosmopolitan society there.

It was Maria's ideal life and she had enjoyed it for six weeks, when, on 2 December, they were astonished to find themselves in the midst of a military coup. In her diary she wrote: '2nd December. Memorable Day. Awoke to find Paris full of military, the Assembly closed, a number of Generals in prison by order of Prince Louis, the sole dictator for time, troops riding about Tuileries all day. 3rd. Military infesting every place, quiet for the present, but who knows what the morrow will bring forth. Dined with Mackenzies, met Miss Sterling, Mr Fraser, and Wilkins came in evening, all troops in Champs Élysées looked beautiful. 4th. Went to see Mr Geffuhle in morning, met crowds of low faces across the Boulevards in returning. Woman rushed and told me it was impossible to pass on Boulevards – shopkeepers shutting up shops, consternation on every face, a mass of hands coming from Porte St Denis, and Soldiers looking very warlike, approaching to meet them. I asked a shopkeeper what they were going to do. "Qu'es ce qu'on va faire? On va se battre." was the answer. We hurried home, then all the afternoon cannonading terrible – I saw the ambulance carried about for wounded prisoners shot at night.

Mr Hey dined with us.' The excitement must have upset her a little, even though the disturbance was not enough to stop socialising, because the next entry is also dated the 4th, but the worst was over, and she writes: 'Paris quiet, but people look terrified, one and all, much military going about – wet day.' The next day they 'went in a carriage to see where the barricades had been, down to the Bastille – quantities of houses perforated by cannon.' Two days after that they went to the Élysée to be introduced by Lord Normanby to the President, who spoke twice to them, and the only sign of the recent upheaval was 'a mass of military and very few ladies present.' So ended Maria's taste of revolution.

We tend to think of nineteenth century travel as not only leisurely but peaceful but, from these accounts of family travel, it seems that peacefulness depended on where you were at what particular time. Unrest was certainly very localised compared with what we have since experienced, but these accounts remind one that there was nearly always trouble somewhere. The Farquhars understandably felt the discomforts of travel in France in 1815, but Walter and Katherine were inconvenienced by the 'swarthy Egyptian soldier with his Damascus blade' in Thrace in 1844, and in 1847 Maria, safe in Italy, records 'Terrible news from France, the King fled, Republic declared' and, a few weeks later: 'War declared against the Austrians by Milanese – recruits going off from here, great joy evinced.' It was in 1851 that she was caught up in the trouble in Paris and, in 1854, the Cosways noted, with displeasure, the Austrian presence in Northern Italy. The travellers never apparently suffered more than inconvenience; they never actually had to cancel dinner engagements, but still there was nothing like universal peace.

Georgina and Helen Cosway – 1854-1855

When the Cosways set out on their travels in the autumn of 1853, it was Nina who kept the diary even though she was the invalid for whose sake the journey was undertaken. Lady Cosway, like Lady Farquhar, had suffered from illness and bereavement and she was setting out now in a state of depression and anxiety, but she had one comfort denied to Lady Farquhar, for her son was able to go with her as guide and courier to the family party.

It was late in October when the family, Lady Cosway, her son Halliday and her daughters, Nina, Helen and Marion, set out from Cowes, and Nina started her *Memoranda* on a sketching pad with marbled covers. The diary is clearly and neatly written, for which one is grateful and the ideas in it are also clear, but they are noticeably circumscribed. One remembers that she was weak and ill and it is amazing that she was able to write at all during a journey that must have been cruelly exhausting for even the most robust of people. One remembers, too, that during four years of illness her life must necessarily have been limited, but it is not querulousness or ignorance that depresses, but the dogmatic certainty with which she expresses her ideas.

Travel is said to broaden the mind and the Cosways were ready to observe new and different sights but at least as far as the females were concerned, one feels that had there been any possibility of their basic beliefs, moral, religious or patriotic, being modified in any way, they probably would not have trusted themselves in foreign parts. Nina's health was at stake but, even so, the soul is more important than the body. As it was, there seemed to be no danger. Nina was, above all, a moralist, and travel abroad gave her ample scope to indulge herself.

In contrast to most other excursions abroad, theirs went very smoothly at first and they were in Rouen only the day after they left Cowes. After a brief description of the town 'interesting to English travellers for its historic associations', she really gets into her stride at the cathedral: 'The Cathedral is a magnificent building, and it is said to have been founded as early as 260. The ironwork is beautifully delicate, and the lofty arches, when filled with the strain of sacred music, must indeed appeal to the senses and produce a chastened feeling of awe and veneration. There were several confessionals, and a passage leading to dungeons, whence the penitent never returned, who once passed that portal; what records of human crime and woe, what vows of continued holiness – what deeds of wrong and injustice, those silent walls had witnessed, in days gone by, is known only to Him, who formed us with such mysterious capacities for suffering and enjoyment: but this much is certain, that few darker pages in this world's sad story, of private sorrow and misery, could be found than is unwritten in the monuments of the past. The review is mournful and humiliating to our proud nature and we, who own a purer faith, ought to strive earnestly to work out under

Providence those views for the infinite progression of our moral being, which He has entrusted to us, as depositaries of a true and Scriptural creed.' In her mind, where there are confessionals, there are almost certainly dungeons! It is altogether rather alarming to contemplate the results of mixing ardent Evangelicalism and patriotism with the Gothic novel.

After this assertion of English superiority, she is in difficulties straight away with Joan of Arc for, having stated that 'La Place de la Pucelle cannot fail to recall one of the most brilliant passages in English History' she unluckily remembers that this particular passage was 'stained' with 'an unworthy use of the Conqueror's power' and she can only resolve the difficulty by concluding that 'Great allowance must be made for the barbarous policy of that day which could execute a woman for devotion to her mission and her country.' In fact, the English were always better, although not as much better as they are now!

They left Rouen quite soon and travelled by train to Paris through a 'lovely part of France which reminds one of Stroud and its environs' but, even then, although the journey was so much quicker and easier than for the previous generation, she had her criticism: 'The speed is much slower than in England, even of the fast trains, and the extravagant waste of time would never be tolerated by us. The officials seem quite astonished at English impatience and wonder how you can think the loss of perhaps two hrs. a matter of any consequence.' It seems a pity for general détente that they felt impelled to share their criticism with the officials even if, no doubt, they meant only to give them a goal to strive towards.

Notre Dame was a disappointment after Rouen. She records: 'Visited Notre Dame on the Isle of St Louis, erected in the 12th century. It has two majestic towers and the floor is of marble. The altar is beautifully carved and in a niche is a fine group representing the Descent from the Cross. There are 120 pillars but their form did not please me and altogether the whole structure and especially the roof and windows are, to my taste, far inferior to the Cathedral at Rouen. But this opinion is doubtless heretical. Notre Dame strikes me as not possessing that mellowed character and softened light and shade which is peculiarly appropriate to religious solemnities.' Maria might well have felt the same, but she would have tried to find out why!

The Louvre was much more worthwhile and she felt well repaid for four hours of fatigue. Murillo, Guido, Raphael, Claude Lorrain, Canaletto and Poussin were singled out, and she particularly admired Poussin's picture of the *Deluge* because it gave 'that darkness visibility which must have existed at such a crisis and the eye was not distracted by the multitude of groups generally depicted in subjects of this sort.' Even here there were signs of foreign inefficiency for the references in the catalogue were 'so badly arranged that it is very difficult to ascertain anything correctly.'

Père la Chaise was the main object of the next day's sightseeing. In her own words, it was: 'A vast human wheat field where lie the remains of many generations, waiting till what was once sown in dishonour shall be raised to glory, and heavenly reapers gather in the world's last harvest. The thought is solemn, and while we gaze on the sleeping ashes, it is difficult to believe that these very men were once instinct with life and performed their part with as much eagerness in their day as we do now. The monuments appear very poor, and there was great want of elegance in sculpture: most of them being little square buildings with name, age, and date inscribed. Many were decorated with everlastings, but on none could I trace the slightest recognition of that Hope in a glorious Resurrection which is a remarkable feature in our English Cemeteries. Not one word of Scripture, or anything which could show that Xtians and not Gentiles, reposed around. The little images were more like heathen deities than civilised artistic productions and altogether I was much disappointed in this celebrated spot. Yet the clumps of cypress and cedar gave a graceful shade and the flowers, so carefully tended, were meet emblems of human frailty.'

They spent a tiring day going by rail to Châlons and then by boat down the Saône to Avignon and on by rail again to Marseilles, where they boarded the steamer *Marie Antoinette* bound for Genoa. They were 'tiresome days of hurry and fatigue' and the river boat was dirty and uncomfortable, although the assemblage of different nationalities on it provided interest. By contrast, the sea voyage was irritatingly slow, taking two days instead of one. It is, therefore, understandable that an invalid had not much energy to spare for recording the beauties of the landscape but, still one senses that, as with Maria, landscape had much less of a direct impact on her than on Walter and Sybella. Steaming down towards Valence, she records: 'The banks to the water's edge, very beautiful. Lofty hills of varied forms, some vine–clad, others naked and barren, rose suddenly to view, and many a ruined castle, with its tale of feudal times, and many a natural fortress, greeted the eye. Several picturesque towns with handsome bridges were seen, but we only stopped a few minutes at each of these places to land merchandise.' Fog delayed their start from Lyons but, when it cleared, there was revealed 'a charming landscape to our admiring gaze. Alps in the distance and tree-covered islands, varied the scene, and the whole way from Lyons to Avignon, repays much fatigue.' It seems a slightly dutiful catalogue, automatic in the same way that, by now, a ruined castle automatically 'told tales of feudal times.' The spectacular road from Genoa via the Riviera di Levante to Spezia could not fail to arouse enthusiasm. Going up the Bracco Pass in the early morning, she says: 'The ascent was tedious but beautiful and the view exceedingly fine. Hills upon hills, clad with the feathery olive whose green contrasted well with the rich red glow of the chestnut, now decked in Autumn tints, and these again giving place to the dark pine, till, as we reached the summit, stunted grass alone showed a colder region, and, at last, nothing could be seen but the rugged rock, with its red and white strata.' She was certainly not indifferent to her surroundings, and yet, reading through the whole of her short diary, one gets the feeling that, compared with Sybella Farquhar's reactions, some of the freshness and excitement of nature had worn off and, as with Maria, people and their capabilities were more important.

The railways cannot be extended quickly enough for her taste; she is much more interested in getting there, wherever 'there' is, than in stopping the carriage here and there to admire chance-met beauties. Even in Old Fiesole where Walter would have rhapsodised about the ancients Nina notes 'the almost unbroken line of wall ... still gives proof of the wonderful powers of the Etruscans in raising heavy weights ... There are various holes and apertures and we long to ascertain if the builders possessed any knowledge of the pulley and lever.'! Sybella might well not have known what pulleys and levers were but, by now, the age of engineering was really making itself felt.

Genoa, Pisa, Florence and Perugia were, of course, visited on the way and guidebook descriptions of buildings and pictures dutifully drawn up. As with Maria, it is feeling and expression that recommend a picture. In the Pitti Palace she admired

Guido's picture of Cleopatra with the asp on her pillow for its beauty of expression, but was most impressed by the 'gem of the collection', the Madonna della Seggiola. In the Tribune she noted that Correggio's Madonna was 'very sweet and in his best style', but was offended by a Venus by Titian 'remarkable for its accuracy and naturalness tho' displeasing for its indelicacy.' At the end of her tour, after admiring 'the passion and beauty' of the group of Niobe and her children, she concludes: 'I prefer a *first-rate* statue to a picture of equal merit, but inferior paintings are generally better than inferior sculpture and there are fewer chefs-d'oeuvre in the one class than in the other.'

Already, in Pisa and Florence, she had been too weak to climb any steps and had often to curtail her sightseeing because of fatigue. After four days of hard travel and very early rising, they reached Foligno where she was 'quite laid up' but, in spite of this, they pressed on next day to Terni where 'another fit of illness overtook me.' Still they went on through beautiful country 'reminding us often of North Devon' and entered Rome by the old Flaminian Way. The 'Eternal City' naturally roused predictable musings when she exchanged 'the hurry and bustle for the silent chamber', but she concludes: 'And yet my impressions are not now what they would have been in the days of early youth, but all is seen through the chastened medium of recent sorrow and that mellowed feeling that added years generally bring to a thoughtful spirit.' She was not yet twenty-one!

The cruel discomforts of this ceaseless travel had been too much for her; no wonder she longed for more and better railways! She rapidly worsened and died in Rome. Her tombstone still stands, remarkably well preserved, in the Protestant Cemetery and one cannot help feeling that, in a small way, it is also the tombstone of many of the grander ideas of the late eighteenth and early nineteenth centuries. In her earnest but limited mind, religious revival had made her one of the chosen few, cutting her off spiritually from most of the rest of the world: the exuberant patriotism that came with victory had turned into a narrow 'we are the best'; the Gothic revival severely limits her choice of 'proper' ecclesiastical buildings; the medieval revival becomes an affair of dungeons and religious oppression and even the grandest scenery is composed into a pretty picture. As with Maria, 'heart' is important, but it tends to be of the sweet variety, whether it is the 'sweet expression' of the Madonna or the 'pretty thought' of praying for the 'Government of the country where we sojourn next after our own Royal Family.' The fact that most of her sentiments are not thought out, but strung together as seemed proper for the occasion, can be no consolation for the architects of spiritual and aesthetic revolution and revival. Guiltily, one reminds oneself repeatedly of the narrowing effects of a long illness and the blessing of a strong faith to one about to die, but one must also hope that her ascending spirit found that the angels were Protestant English.

How long the rest of the party lingered in Rome is not recorded, but they did continue their proposed travels. In May of the following year, Helen, a self-assured young lady of twenty-four, starts a diary as they leave Naples for Leghorn, travelling by sea to avoid Rome. She writes with as much clarity, both in handwriting and style, as her sister. Her opinions are startlingly the same and her tendency to moralising as strong, but she writes with the energy that comes no doubt, from a healthy body and stronger mind and she has the saving grace of a sarcastic sense of humour as well as a cheerfully sharp eye for the foibles of others. She also writes well and uses her words with economy, so that her record makes more entertaining reading than Nina's even if, retrospectively, one would sometimes like to shake her.

At every stop they faithfully visit the places of interest and this invariably means the picture galleries and churches. She admires the same sort of pictures as Nina, always noting expression, particularly of sweetness or devotion, but, being a well-organised person, she makes neat lists of pictures labelled 'These are the pictures that pleased me most.' As far as churches are concerned, she also likes simplicity and is continually offended by the gilding and gaudiness to be found so regrettably often in Italian churches, and she refers to 'dim religious light' with distressing frequency. Milan is the first cathedral that seems to her to possess 'A real character of solemnity' which she finds so rare in Italian churches. At the end of her tour, visiting her last foreign building, the cathedral at Boulogne, she confesses to 'tourists' disease': 'It is not easy to keep distinct in one's mind the different styles of each edifice we have seen. A knowledge of Architecture would be essential to the appreciation of their respective merits: we must therefore rest content with a general idea.' Still, she is quite certain about what she likes: 'Nothing, I own, pleases me so well for a sacred Structure as the Gothic. The pointed arch, massive pillars, and general solemnity, enhanced by the "dim, religious light" which pervades the whole, appears to me more suited, in its grand simplicity to the worship of One who is a spirit, than a more brilliant and gorgeous style.' Here again, Maria would probably have agreed with her conclusion, although she would have tried harder to find out why she felt this and she would not have been content with a general idea, but would have struggled to keep places distinct in her mind by studying architecture as exhaustively as possible.

Helen is as aggressively Protestant as her sister, noting when they are able to have a Sunday service and when, to the shame of the place in which they are staying, there is no proper provision. For the most part she thoroughly approved of Turin, but it fell short in one respect and she wrote indignantly: 'To our great disappointment we found no English Service. It is a great shame of our Government not to provide a Chaplain wherever we have an Ambassador. How must the foreigners think we regard our religion, when they see our representative sent out, without any provision for his religious worship?'

When she is fortunate enough to be able to attend an English service she does not comment on the priest or the sermon, as Maria did, or even, like Nina, on the appositeness of the psalms but, if she is happy with the form rather than the content of a service, she is just as apt as Nina to moralise on other occasions. The Campo Santo at Bologna rouses almost the same feelings in her as Père la Chaise did in Nina, although she does not actually mention a 'human wheatfield' and she does show her stronger practical streak: 'We also went to the Campo Santo. Like all foreign Cemeteries it is without the town: it would be well in this aspect if we followed the same practice. It is on a very large scale. Most of the Monuments along the cloisters are simply designs at present, but the different families are to have them executed in marble. This Cemetery was formed fifty years ago, since which time 180,000 persons have been interred: two generations, the population being now 90,000. This lays in vivid colours before us the frailty and shortness of human life, yet how each individual and generation act as if *they* were to abide for ever. Were a Being from another world to visit us, surely he would imagine men immortal by the intenseness with which they are absorbed with the things of Time. Lead him from the whirl of life within, to this spot without the walls, and tell him fifty years since, all here were instinct with life, double the number you have just seen now, they have entered a state that will last forever, for which the life you see is the preparation. Would not his first enquiry be How men could best prepare for eternity? And when told how comparatively few thought about it all, would he not point with astonishment to the graves around him, and ask the solemn question, your fathers, where are they ...?'

Helen's religion was strongly laced with patriotism; her patriotism was based on a love of freedom of the Byronic type. Sardinia was her favourite Italian state because 'Her liberal spirit is allowed to raise its head', and this 'gives the people a strong sympathy with the English. So much do they imitate us in our free sentiments that many of the other states prohibit their subjects entering so dangerous an atmosphere.' She was very much impressed by Turin, even though there was no English church. They arrived just in time for the celebration of the sixth anniversary of the Constitution so the town was crowded but the people were orderly, even without the presence of soldiers. 'And what,' she asks rhetorically, 'is the result of this new system? We were told that since a Constitution was granted and freedom of sentiment allowed, they no longer fear a crowd: the people, contented, conducted themselves quietly, dispersed by 11 p.m. and for the last six years no one has made any disturbance on such festive occasions.' It does not actually sound much fun, even though the next day there were Allegorical Cars parading the streets in celebration.

Of course, Protestant freedom was the most stirring and, later in her travels, as she floats along the Rhine, she is roused more by thoughts of Luther than of chivalry. True, she is moved, as she nears Cologne, to write: 'Hills clothed with verdure, frequently vine-clad, descended in varied form to the water's edge. While many an ancient Castle, well known in Historic or Fairy lore, frowned o'er the rapidly winding Rhine. Where are the Feudal Barons and fair Maids who once inhabited these crag-built Fortresses? How many a tale of Chivalry, alas, too often of cruelty, might those walls relate!' But this is cool and automatic compared with her earlier feelings on passing Spiers and Worms: 'Their connection with History,' she says, 'not their situation, inspires them with interest, an interest to a Protestant of the highest nature and perhaps never more deeply felt than after seeing the nature and results of the Faith whose corruptions

Luther so vehemently withstood. Within those walls, the Gospel trumpet, so long rendered mute by the traditions which usurped its place, sounded a note which has found an echo in all succeeding generations. A light was re-kindled which shall shine brighter and brighter to the end of time.' The language is as stereotyped as that she uses about castles and chivalry, but it is much more deeply felt!

Naturally, with these strong sentiments, Chillon proved of more than usual interest, for it had a medieval castle with the very best dungeons and picturesque scenery thrown in as well; then, to crown all, there was Byron's poem. Here were all her enthusiasms in one place, sealed with poetic approval: five and a half pages of her diary are applied to them. Naturally, she gives a good deal of space to the description of the dungeon in which Bonivard was imprisoned and quotes: 'Chillon, Thy prison is a holy place ...' but she is equally circumstantial about the other dungeons. She describes, too, the pulley used to drop victims and dislocate their shoulders and the room with the trap-door in the floor through which prisoners were dropped on to spikes below. One is almost cheered by her ghoulish enjoyment as evidence of normal frailty, but she climbs quickly back to her platform of moral rectitude and rounds off this entry with: 'Within the walls where such tragedies were enacted were the apartments of the Duke and Duchess of Savoy. The former had a secret door by which to escape to the dungeons if surprised by any enemies. The fears which suggested such a refuge were the clear tokens of a guilty conscience – Doubtless many an innocent victim found more peace of mind in his lonely dungeon dimly lighted by the reflection of the sun's rays on the blue lake, through the narrow slit, than many a Duke in that upper chamber, haunted by the thought of a coming retribution for his deeds of tyranny.' Considering the dungeons, which she describes so vividly, one takes leave to doubt this, but one can almost see her folding her hands, and pursing her mouth in an expression of proper disapproval.

It is interesting to notice how often poetry is used to help description in Nina's and Helen's diaries, a habit which the older diaries do not seem to have acquired. It is not only Chillon which merits a quotation from Helen; the sight of the Eiger, Monnck, Jungfrau and Finsteraarhorn 'recall the lines of the poet':

Above me are the Alps
The Palaces of Nature, whose vast walls
Have pinnacled in clouds their snowy scalps
And throned Eternity in icy halls
Of cold sublimity, where forms and falls
The avalanche, the thunderbolt of snow.
All that expands the spirit, yet appals
Gather around these summits, as to show
How Earth may pierce to Heaven, yet leave
Vain man below.

and Byron again comes to her aid at Waterloo where she rounds off her description with a few lines from *Childe Harold*:

Last noon beheld them full of lusty life,
Last eve in Beauties circle proudly gay
The midnight brought the signal sound of strife,
The morn the marshalling in arms – the day
Battle's magnificently stern array;
The thunder clouds close o'er it which when rent
The earth is covered thick with other clay
Which her own clay shall cover, heaped and spent,
Rider and horse, friend, foe – in one red burial blent.

Nina is moved to quote from Michelangelo's *Morning and Night, Dawn and Twilight*. They can never be forgotten, she says, and are best described in the words of the poet:

Nor then forget the Chamber of the Dead
Where the gigantic shapes of Night and Day
Turned into stone, rest everlastingly.

and she goes on for fourteen more lines! It leaves one wondering if they had all these apposite quotations off by heart and ready to apply or if they carried their pocket poets with them as well as their *Murray's Guides*. It is very impressive but also gives a slightly second-hand air to their impressions.

It is probably quite wrong to conclude that, compared with the previous generation, they were not really much impressed by the wilder forms of nature. Indeed, it could probably be argued that the love of nature in its grander manifestations had become so much part of their lives and their creeds that they might have felt deprived, if shut away from it. Helen is, in fact, quite capable of giving an immediate description of natural beauty. Here is her account of driving along the valley of the Arc: 'The road was wild and beautiful; at one part it ascends high above the river, while the deep gorge forms a natural rampart round Fort Sesseillon, the stronghold which guards the passage to Italy. We stopped at Modane where we found a simple but clean country Inn. 18th. Continued in this lovely valley, containing every variety of scenery. Mountains wild and grand, and then others wooded to their summit: the valley now widening, now contracted to a narrow gorge, only to break out into a richer and larger extent of verdure, while beneath, the Arc tumbled and foamed as it rushed along its rocky bed.' The main difference seems to be that by this time so much had been written and read on the subject that the educated traveller was well schooled in admiration. Not only was she often betrayed into comparing famous places rather as though the beauty had been laid on in much the same way as the hotels, but she may also have been most conscious that the professional pen had covered the situation exhaustively: it might also seem presumptuous to undertake too much amateur description without, at least, referring to 'greater pens than mine.'

The differences between Sybella's and Helen's reactions are most obvious when one reads their description of visits to the same places. In due course, the Cosway family made their way to the Alps. Sybella was transported by the 'exquisite beauty of the country' as she began the ascent to them and she was also excited by the danger of the road. Helen was so deeply moved that she overflowed into moralising: 'Not a zephyr ruffled the placid bosom of the waters, which reflected in their clear mirror the "Alps which on Alps arise", their snowy crests shimmering bright and dazzling with the early sunlight. It was a sunny and happy scene: not an unapt picture of human life. In its early morning often joyous yet, if I may so speak, with a calm deep joy; not the mirth of exuberant spirits only, but the feeling of unknown powers springing into being. The fair prospect may, and probably will, be clouded but, as evening draws on, we may hope that as o'er the landscape steals a peaceful calm, even so those who have been led to the only abiding Source of peace may realise the truth, "At evening time it shall be light".' One is almost betrayed into a fervent 'amen'.

Helen was naturally quite as energetic and adventurous as Sybella, but she was sadly restricted by the physical capabilities of Mama and Marion. Right at the beginning of her diary she records her disappointment at having to go by boat instead of through the Apennines which were 'so unfrequented that the nightly accommodation was most dubious and also the nature of the Post horses that we might get.' In view of this 'Mama therefore thought it better to choose the sea. I confess that for myself I much regretted the decision as the beauty of the mountain scenery would have compensated for much discomfort.' She was disappointed again in the Alps: 'I had much wished,' she writes, 'to visit Grindelwald by crossing the Wengen-Alp that I might have at least one mountain expedition to remember; but it was too great an undertaking for Mama and Marion.' So she had to be content with a drive through the valley. When they reached Grindelwald, however, she and Halliday were at least able to go on the lower of the two glaciers. Again, one thinks of Sybella's excitement at first seeing a glacier: 'There are immense cracks or crevices in these Glaciers which are frightful to look down, they are yawning gulfs of a bluish colour.' And again on the Mer de Glace: 'I could not help shuddering to see how we were surrounded by yawning bottomless precipices of ice, and where the most trifling imprudence or accident might have precipitated us.' Here is Helen's account: 'The accumulation of soil renders the lower part less bright and pure than could be wished; but as you ascend the ice retains its picturesque hue. The pale blue tint as you gaze down some deep crevasse is almost ethereal in its tenderness. This field of ice may give, I suppose, some faint idea of the Arctic region, judging at least from pictures. It is a merciful provision of the Creator that these seas of ice must disappear as they reach a lower level, generally giving birth to some fertilizing stream. Were it otherwise, what fearful devastation would they occasion in their onward progress. In all the scenes of nature we are constantly led to adore the wisdom which planned the whole. It was not easy, even with the guide's assistance, to walk on the unequal surface. Some new Boots told what unkind treatment *they* considered it.' This reads like a lesson in how to put a glacier in its place! She continues: 'Numbers of children besieged us with entreaties to purchase their little chalets. It was amusing to hear how they outdid each other in their desire to procure purchasers.' One remembers the peasants selling minerals from Mont Blanc in Sybella's day and wonders, in passing, what this cult of the simple grandeur of the mountains was doing to the local inhabitants' native simplicity.

Of course, they moved on from here to Lauterbrunnen to see the Staubbach. To Sybella it was a perfect landscape and 'the most picturesque situation in the world.' Here is Helen on the subject: 'The chief of these falls is the well-known Staubbach (literally Dust-stream). It falls from a height of between 800 and 900 feet. It is hardly a *water*fall, as the small body of water which forms it is shivered into spray, long e're it reaches the bottom. Byron has compared it to the tail of a white horse streaming in the wind. We were not quite satisfied with this comparison. To me it appeared rather like some sprite from fairy regions lost amid Alpine summits, who, startled and frightened at the appalling precipice which suddenly arrests its progress, dashes rapidly over, assuming an impalpable form. Mid-way it seeks a resting place which is denied. There is none for it till the depth of the abyss be gained.' According to Maria, this would certainly rank as fancy rather than imagination. At all events, it leaves one feeling that it was perhaps as well that Helen generally left description in the hands of the poets.

Sybella longed to explore any buildings perched on crags and was most disappointed in not being able to visit the Convent of St Bernard. Helen was luckier and was able to make one memorable ascent. Leaving Mama and Marion, she and Halliday rode heavy carthorses up the Abendberg to visit the Cretin Hospital. Even though the director, Dr Guggenbuhl, was away, they were shown every attention by the Matron, and were allowed to make a thorough inspection of the establishment which impressed them greatly. They were not shown the worst cases, but saw about twenty others in 'various stages of improvement'. 'Most of them,' she noted, 'had the conical head and air of vacuity of idiots. But we were told that as the mind opened, their head resumed a better shape. This would rather support the theory of the phrenologists.' She describes two children almost ready to leave for the outer world and then goes on to say: 'There appears to be a difference between the Cretin and the Idiot. In the former, bodily disease affects the mind: in the latter, the mental powers are at fault, while the body is sound and healthy. Consequently the Cretin affords a more hopeful subject for cure than the Idiot.' She records with admiration the patience and kindness of the nurses in this isolated position though, in passing, remarks that at present only women are employed; once there was a master but 'patience is not one of the male virtues and the attempt failed.' She notes how the high pure air was one of the main requisites for treatment and that a great deal of water was used in the form of baths and rounds off her account with the inevitable moral reflection: 'They continue their silent work, unknown and unpraised by the world: no earthly distinction is theirs, but their reward shall be great in Heaven 'for whosoever giveth a cup of cold water to one of these little ones, shall in no wise lose his reward.' Her account is long, but there is no mere curiosity and no ghoulishness; her interest is deeply engaged. She may be deficient in imagination and have to labour at the romantic response, but she has a highly developed social conscience and truly wishes people to be not only Protestant and as nearly as possible English, but also clean, healthy, happy and prosperous. Her natural affinities are with the Victorian reformers.

They made one more excursion that had already been made and recorded by both Sybella and Maria, and this was to Waterloo. Sybella was there very soon after the engagement, Maria went thirty-five years later, and it was thirty-nine years afterwards that Helen made her record, but really more interesting than her own response is the description of how Waterloo itself had been developed as a tourist attraction. It was still too recent to 1815 to be well organised, so Sybella had an uncomfortable time of it, although the souvenir sellers were already on the spot. By the time Maria got there, it was thoroughly tidied up, with transport and the itinerary organised, but, by Helen's visit, it was a very flourishing industry. She starts her description with 'Waterloo, a name which fires the breast of every Briton, was our great attraction in visiting Brussels: and perhaps there was scarcely any spot we have visited which more fully satisfied us than this famous Battle-field. Such numbers of English visit the place that two four-horse Coaches go over daily while another meets them at the village to drive round the field. The idea seems very Cockney and barbarous but it is no bad plan for visitors as the best Guide has been secured.' This guide became quite famous himself; he was a Sergeant Munday who had fought in the great battle, and he obviously did a very good job for, not only did he give 'a tolerably clear idea of the positions of the respective forces' and explain the progress of the battle at the various points, but he knew when to put in a story of personal interest to make it more immediate. In passing the barn at Houguemont he tells of a sergeant who obtained permission to leave his post for a few moments and succeeded in dragging his wounded brother to safety just as the burning roof fell in. 'Amidst such scenes of blood,' reflects Helen, 'it is pleasing to pause a while on a trait like this.' He also told them of 'a singular instance of adherence to supposed duty at a time when self-preservation might have well usurped its place.' The Duke advised the inmates of Houguemont to leave it and take to the forest, which they did, all but a maidservant who insisted on staying, for who else would take care of the pigs and the poultry? There was also a pleasant little anecdote about the Duke coming off his horse, and then they were returned to the village to see the late Sergeant Cotton's Museum of Waterloo Remains which included 'autographs of many celebrated Chiefs' and, finally, there were the souvenirs.

'Some persons,' writes Helen, 'try now to impose on you by offering bullets or bits of iron, just found, probably lately buried for the purpose.' The pattern, still so successful, has already been worked out! Even without the 'few lines from Byron' and typical interpolations such as: 'A few short hours and many a pulse beating high in the hope of victory would be hushed for ever. The turf their winding-sheet, their spirit where?' Helen's is, by far, the longest account for, by now, it had become both important history and glorious legend. She, too, remarks on the Belgian monument; but, while Maria's criticism was primarily aesthetic with moral overtones, Helen's was uncompromisingly moral: 'The original appearance of the field has been in part much altered by the removal of earth to raise the mound surmounted by the Belgic Lion. It certainly had been better taste for those who fled in the hour of danger to avoid creating a monument which only suggests animadversions on their conduct.'

So far, Helen seems the least attractive of the family diarists: her brisk moralising at the slightest opportunity is not pleasing to us now, nor is her aggressive patriotism, but she has other redeeming characteristics and the foremost of these is a detached, dry humour, with which she greets the vicissitudes of travel and the vagaries of other people. Even though the mechanics of travel had changed a good deal since Sybella and Walter were young, there were still many of the same difficulties to endure. There were still many bad and muddy roads and horses and carriages were still just as unreliable. She gives a spirited account of one occasion in Italy, when nothing would go right: 'We took fresh horses, one of ours being ill, and had, fortunately, not cleared the village when a spring broke. In spite of pouring rain, we had to turn out and make the best of our way back to the Inn. A fire was quickly kindled, and we set to work to dry ourselves. No other carriage was to be found but, after an hour's delay, ours was set to rights. But truly, misfortunes never come alone. We had gone but a short distance when our horse declined going on, and showed a great disposition to return. In mountain roads, such conduct was not pleasant, so we had him changed. We got a quiet horse certainly, but a very slow one, so that our fears of being benighted again returned; however, they were not realised, as at Piarroro, about 12 miles from Bologna, the hill ceased and we reached our hotel, the San Marco by 7 p.m.' On another occasion, on their way out of Chambéry, they were more seriously frightened, but this time it was the fault of the driver rather than the horses: 'There is a long hill immediately on quitting the town; whilst ascending, we had a great fright. The driver, while walking, whipped the horses sharply to send them from one side of the road and, having carelessly left the reins, they darted to the opposite side and, before he could check them, we were in the ditch. Providentially, a hedge prevented the carriage going right over, or we might have been seriously hurt. I was outside, looking at Murray, when I found myself rolled over to the other part of the hood. The horses remained quiet, so we all scrambled out, and the carriage was soon set straight. It was a great mercy it was not a precipitous road or a very steep bank.' On their way to Interlaken she remarked: 'The bridge across the Aar was washed away in the inundation of 1851. It is not unlikely, to my mind, that the present one may share the same fate.' Evidently, extensive travel prepared one's mind for the worst!

Dirty inns were another frequent annoyance which all the travellers had met with, but they inadvertently made their presence felt in one of these: 'The 2nd night, at Cigliano, we had very poor accommodation; that is to say, the rooms were very tolerable, but cleanliness was sadly wanting. We created an illumination by setting fire to the window-curtains; fortunately, it did not spread, so the damage was not great.' Then another familiar accident overtook them the next morning. 'We had another breakdown by the wheel coming off, but it occurred in a village which was very obliging, as it could at once be mended.' No wonder she approves, on the whole, of the railway! Towards the end of the tour, she says: 'A railway is certainly very acceptable in an ugly country. Six hours took us from Basle to Strasbourg, a much longer time must have been spent en route formerly with no adequate advantage.' The actual travelling must, at times, have been a severe trial. No wonder Helen writes rather ruefully: 'Undoubtedly, travelling is very trying to the temper. It is not a bad test for many persons, not only in the eyes of others, but giving them a good opportunity of judging themselves ... It is a discipline by which much may be brought to light which had probably remained unthought of, perhaps unknown, amidst the more routine duties of daily life!' There is, however, one aspect of travel which is rarely mentioned although it is one of the main preoccupations of modern travellers, and that is food, nor do they ever seem to suffer from the stomach upsets which we expect and guard against. The only time that Helen mentions food is in her account of her visit to the Cretin Hospital, when the kind Matron 'insisted on our taking some refreshment and thinking to avoid giving trouble we chose some milk and bread. I had cause to repent my choice. The milk which was warmed was fearfully *goaty*, and there we were condemned to drink a tumblerful. From experience I can advise others never to try hot goat's milk' – but there did not seem to be any ill-effects!

In spite of the difficulties of travel, and in spite of having to take in so many 'places of interest' in rapid succession, she still has an eye for small amusements on the way. She describes the costumes of the peasants in some of the cantons, remarking that a slim figure is an essential for that of Berne. In Berne, too, she remarks that you are never allowed to forget whence the name originated 'as on every side this animal has its representative in some way or other.' In Milan she is amused to see that, on the Arco della Pace, a copy of the Arch of Constantine, the desire for verisimilitude has led the sculptor to represent Talleyrand, Metternich and Lord Aberdeen 'in the attire of Grecian sages and warriors' and one wonders if she was similarly amused by the bust of Uncle Walter draped in a toga in the hall at Glenthorne.

She seemed quite ready to talk to people and, in spite of a heavy swell and the resultant sickness, enjoyed the crowds on the steamer when they left Naples and she began her diary. They shared their cabin with 'A nice old Swiss lady and two Americans of whose manners and habits I cannot say much.' But she said, 'It is fair to add that the gentlemen of their party were very superior and we found them very agreeable companions.' At the end of the journey, on the way from Aix-la-Chapelle to Brussels, they met another American who was 'most gentlemanly and polite.' Again, she records her prejudice against American ladies, finding them lacking in manners and overbearing, but she thoroughly enjoyed hearing from the polite gentleman about the glories of America: 'The magnificence of their Steamers and Hotels,' she exclaims, 'was something astonishing.'

Her interest in people and her way of describing bustle and crowds suggests that she has some of the genial energy of Uncle Walter. Even when exhausted at the end of the long tour they have to put up with the last straw of a bad Channel crossing, she is irrepressible: 'The moment we quitted Boulogne, we were warned by sundry rolls and tossings that we should not probably escape the penalty crossing the Channel usually involved. In a few minutes most of the passengers in the most grotesque style lay stretched out on deck. Mama, I think, was the only Lady who seemed quite at ease. Poor Mrs Butter (the Butter family were friends they had met in Switzerland) at once yielded to her fate. Harry and I just succeeded in avoiding the last stage. Marion and May could not hold out. It was thought an excellent passage. Doubtless it might have been worse but it was far from a pleasant sail. As the vessel hauled alongside of Folkestone quay, a group of ghostlike faces suddenly rose from the deck. We must have afforded a melancholy specimen of the effect of a sea voyage to the many spectators on shore. At best the sea to most is an evil, a penalty which those who determine on a Continental tour must pay. "What can't be cured must be endured" is the only maxim for such occasions!' It is a pity, after this, that she feels compelled to round off her journal with a little more moralising: 'This is my *own*, my *native* Land. A Land possessing a pure religion so free from the superstitions found elsewhere, a free Constitution and an integrity and honour above her Fellows. Well may she deserve our love! May we as a Nation take heed and walk circumspectly lest we lose the high privileges committed to us. While gratefully acknowledging our many advantages may we be faithful to our high position remembering that "unto whomsoever much is given, of them shall much be required".' One is tempted to say hopefully that the girl who wrote the lively sharp comments is the 'real' Helen and that the moralising is put in because it was the fashion and she felt she ought, but this is not true; the two aspects existed side by side, and were equally 'true'.

As she grew older, she became, if anything, more evangelical and one of the churchmen she most admired was Dr Vaughan, renowned for being *very* low'. She was a tiny, small-featured lady, a type much admired by the Victorians, but she never married. Nevertheless, she was never the sort of 'optional extra' that many maiden aunts were supposed to become. She managed her own and other people's business with such firmness that she was known to the next generation as *The* Aunt, although they also loved her. There was time also for good works and, in any household where she had influence, family prayers were never missed. Her favourite prayer was that for the Church Militant.

Looking back through these diaries, one realises that Maria, Nina and Helen are alike in their difference from Sybella and Walter. Nature, though important, had lost its near-mystical significance and Man had become much more important: he was God's highest creation, and the rest of the natural creation was devoted to justifying God's way to Man. Religion had also become more important and much more personal and the heart, properly prepared, was a more reliable guide than the mind. The Middle Ages rather than classical times had become 'antiquity' and, as ideas and enthusiasms changed, so did vocabulary. When one compares Maria and Helen, however, one realises that they are so different from each other that one wonders how well they ever understood one another, even when, later in life, they spent a great deal of time together. Maria, naturally endowed with a restless and complicated intellect, spent a good deal of time trying to cultivate the simplicity of the heart, looking into her own and finding it puzzlingly complicated. Nina and Helen were, in fact, the first of this group of people who seemed to spend no time at all searching for simplicity: they presumably had it! They approved of simple church architecture as a meet expression of a simple faith. One learned this faith early and stuck to it and, in its light, always putting God first, one did one's best for one's fellow creatures.

It is always difficult to determine how much individual characters are shaped by the ideas prevalent at the time, and how much innate characteristics lead people to choose some ideas more than others from those available. The interaction is bound to be complicated. The travels recorded in these journals were undertaken for different reasons: Sybella's and Walter's for pleasure and amusement; Maria's and the Cosways' in search of health and as a diversion from grief, so they are bound to be different in atmosphere but, even so, they seem to follow very much the general change of emphasis and attitude in nineteenth century ideas. Gradually, nature, at least of the wilder variety, became less important than humanity, people turned more inward and religion became more a matter of dogma. The atmosphere seemed to grow a little thicker and darker. Ironically, as travel became easier, minds did not become broader. It seemed indeed as if the ordinary person observed foreign ways in order to give shape and identity to their own attitudes. Walter was certainly more a citizen of the world than Nina or Helen and, greatest irony of all, the money-makers of the family, for whom travel was most dangerous and who were basically interested only in preserving their lives while making their fortunes, were probably, of all these people, the most at home at the ends of the earth.

THE NEW SIMPLICITY

After the successful period of retrenchment, when Constance and Aunt Helen had settled back into Glenthorne, life must have seemed, superficially at least, to be very much as it had been in Walter's time and, when Constance's eldest sister came to stay with her family, the young heir to the estate and his sisters, history must have appeared to be repeating itself. Helen, in practical energy and sound business ability, was equal to the solider side of Walter and Katherine rolled into one, while Constance represented the imaginative side of Walter. She must always have been quite as odd as he, although nowhere near as odd as Aunt Marion, and she appeared to have no practical ability whatsoever. Helen's religious convictions were much more strongly evangelical than Walter's or Katherine's but her belief in the necessity for good works made her do what she could for the people on the estate and duty was tempered by kindliness, although, at times, it was probably tinged with asperity.

Constance, being the 'delicate one', was expected to die young and indeed, she did predecease her sisters, dying at the age of eight-eight. She was always vague and unbusinesslike and presumably it had never been thought worthwhile to trouble her short life with trying to give her a sense of reality. Her journey through the world was to be considered only as a brief excursion from Heaven. She may not have taken this view but, in spite of a chronic shortage of money, she always considered herself highly privileged and this, with natural kindness, made her most willing to join her aunt Helen in any philanthropic schemes that they could manage to afford. For the rest, she dipped into works, both prose and poetry, of a generally mystic character, knew the Latin names of every plant in the garden, and, quite simply, adored nature. She had poor sight but was an excellent and entirely fearless horsewoman in her youth and used to astonish and alarm the occasional visitor by galloping down the steepest and roughest hills. Later in life she sometimes frightened the gardener's boy as he was taking a last look round for marauding deer, by flitting ghost-like through the dusky garden, a figure of skeletal thinness, shrouded in a voluminous white nightgown. By day, she would sit composedly on the wet grass admiring what she always referred to as 'The Elementals'. If only she had been beautiful, instead of noticeably plain, she would have been the perfect nineteenth century romantic heroine.

By nature, both Helen and her niece, Constance, seemed to have had, in good measure, that spiritual simplicity which is said to suggest a healthy soul. Walter believed in it, and had a good deal of it, while Maria strove earnestly for it. As their income was always very small, Helen and Constance also had the outward simplicity approved by both moralists and the guardians of aesthetic taste favoured by Walter. They both lived long lives so, by chance, plus some misfortune and mismanagement, modern improvement was impossible and Walter's early-nineteenth-century romantic idea was carried precariously on into the twentieth century.

Outwardly, during the time of Constance's ownership, Glenthorne must have appeared a fairly solid entity but if Simon and William could have observed it, they would have felt both sorrow and anger at the wreckage of their hopes and the dissipation of their life's work. It is true that, owing to one provision in his will, Simon's name still continued in spite of a lack of direct male heirs, but his large fortune had disappeared, having all gone into a tract of remote, poor land, which did not, and could not reasonably be expected to, bring any adequate return for capital outlay. He would have been depressed, too, at the spirit of the place. All the energetic, thrusting acquisitiveness which had gained him a fortune in India and commemorated his name in a bay in Australia had disappeared and there remained only one ageing spinster turned inwards on herself. For the shattering of all his hopes, he would have blamed his son, Walter.

William Cosway would have been, if anything, more angered and disappointed for there was no longer anything to show for his efforts at all. His carefully chosen, sensible and fruitful land had been first neglected and then sold to support a relatively barren tract of Exmoor, and even his name had gone when his son changed it in order to inherit the now hollow-seeming Halliday riches. He, too, would have unhesitatingly blamed Walter. How either of them would have accounted for the continued aberration in Walter's successors is a more difficult subject for conjecture.

They could not have blamed alien blood in the first instance, for the Farquhars seemed to be still in an enviably flourishing condition. As for the call of the wild, Simon and William heard it only if it called loudly of money to be made in order to live more comfortably in civilisation.

If they could observe the situation now, they would be, quite simply, astonished. With the increasing size of cities and the intensifying rush and utilitarianism of life in and around them, the love of the picturesque has become more general than ever before. Indeed, it is probably more often publicly acclaimed as good for the mind, soul and morals than even the Church of England. Exmoor has been declared a National Park and so what remains of the Glenthorne estate has now, as it were, received a certificate to say that it has reached the acknowledged standard of British Beauty. Time, thought and public money are spent on the preservation of the naturalness which Walter so lovingly enhanced and, in some part, created. Most of the agricultural part of the estate has been sold, but the tracts surrounding the house, considered by the Simons and Williams of the world to be useless, are now known as an amenity and discreet signposts point the way along the paths that Walter had made with so much labour and expense, so that anyone with strong legs may safely enjoy the solitude of apparently untrodden ways. It is perhaps a comforting consideration that, whatever money or thought, public or private, may or may not be spent on this area, it is so wildly picturesque in the original meaning of the word that its own intransigence will preserve it. Meanwhile, the Reverend Walter Halliday, the family liability, is considered by some to have been, inadvertently perhaps, a public benefactor, and certainly the only remarkable member of an otherwise ordinary family. His house, the domestic expression of his philosophy, has a more problematical future. It still sits composedly on its ledge, presently well cared for. Ultimately, however, it is too big and too isolated for sensible private living; too small and too isolated for institutional purposes. At the worst, however, it will make a most romantic ruin.

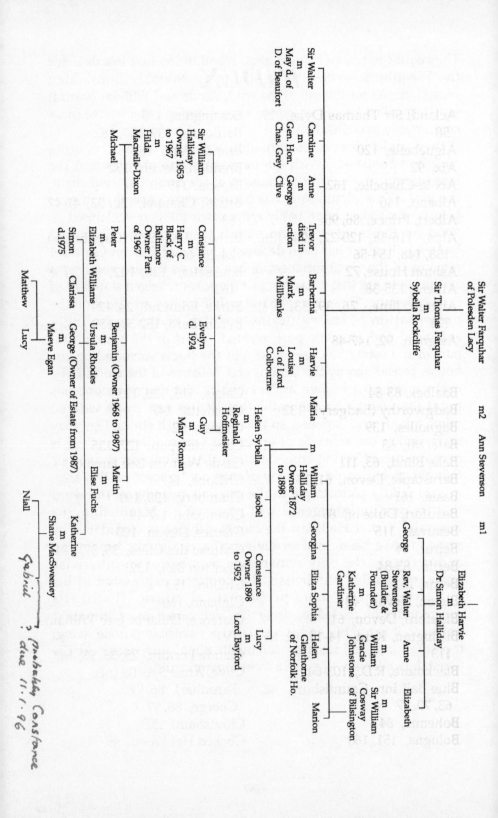

INDEX

172